1190M London   8/P £5-

WALKING LONDON'S
WATERWAYS

WALKING LONDON'S WATERWAYS

Bryan Fairfax

David & Charles
Newton Abbot   London   North Pomfret (Vt)

The maps were drawn by Ethan Danielson, and the line
illustrations by Ken Hatts (from the author's photographs)

British Library Cataloguing in Publication Data
Fairfax, Bryan
Walking London's waterways.
1. Waterways—England—London 2. London
—Description—1951–
I. Title
914.21'04858   DA684.25

ISBN 0-7153-8584-4

Phototypeset by ABM Typographics Limited
and printed in Great Britain
by A. Wheaton & Co. Ltd., Exeter
for David & Charles (Publishers) Limited
Brunel House   Newton Abbot   Devon

Published in the United States of America
by David & Charles Inc
North Pomfret   Vermont 05053   USA

CONTENTS

INTRODUCTION

Exploring London's rivers has grown enormously in recent years and this book shows you how easy it is to get to them. Detailed information is given on public transport for each walk, and a variety of starting and stopping places makes it possible for walkers to adapt the routes to suit themselves. Walks can be varied by doing them in the reverse direction – or by going there and back. It is surprising how different a river looks when viewed one way and then another. Guide maps plot the route, and the relevant Ordnance Survey map is given for each walk.

Official response to this growing interest has been to open up many access points and to restore towpaths. Areas are being landscaped and places of beauty and of historic importance are being preserved. There is an air of optimism about the way in which London's rivers are changing over from their former commercial use to a new social and recreational role and, as a measure of success, they have become a focal point for popular attention and affection.

The Thames itself is the subject of several walks, and includes one of Europe's newest and most imaginative developments – London's old riverside port. Both north and south London are featured – major tributaries and secluded brooks – and all are accessible from main rail and bus routes.

The majority of the walks pass through areas of seclusion and tranquillity so a knapsack with your own refreshment is an advisable standby, but you can always take advantage of pubs when they are open. Photographers and birdwatchers will find ample subjects for their interest and should be equipped accordingly. Make sure that shoes are not only comfortable but are also waterproof and well laced: even in dry weather a

7

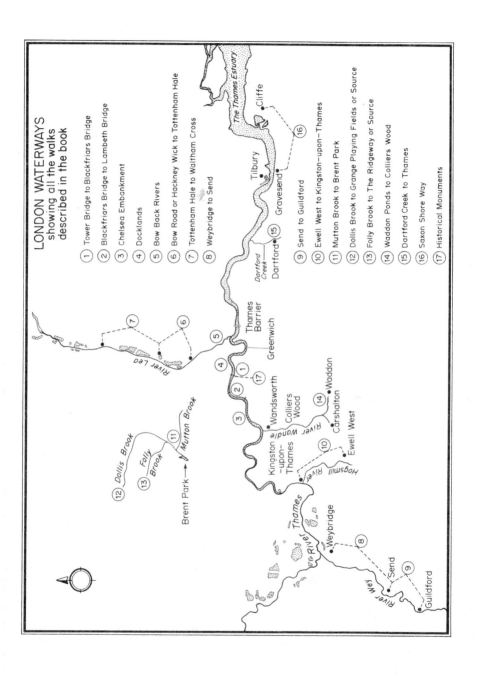

LONDON WATERWAYS
showing all the walks
described in the book

1. Tower Bridge to Blackfriars Bridge
2. Blackfriars Bridge to Lambeth Bridge
3. Chelsea Embankment
4. Docklands
5. Bow Back Rivers
6. Bow Road or Hackney Wick to Tottenham Hale
7. Tottenham Hale to Waltham Cross
8. Weybridge to Send
9. Send to Guildford
10. Ewell West to Kingston-upon-Thames
11. Mutton Brook to Brent Park
12. Dollis Brook to Grange Playing Fields or Source
13. Folly Brook to The Ridgeway or Source
14. Waddon Ponds to Colliers Wood
15. Dartford Creek to Thames
16. Saxon Shore Way
17. Historical Monuments

towpath can have its muddy patches. Winter walking can be delightful along a river: tree-lined banks cut down the wind and the intimate scale of the scenery is not spoilt by hazy conditions.

An Ordnance Survey map will help you to get the most out of your walks but (with the exception of Walks 9 and 16) they are all contained within the Master A–Z London street map.

Finally, do respect the traditions of the countryside. Be careful of fire, close gates and leave no litter. Remember that every bit of land has its owner.

Walk 1: Tower Bridge to Blackfriars Bridge

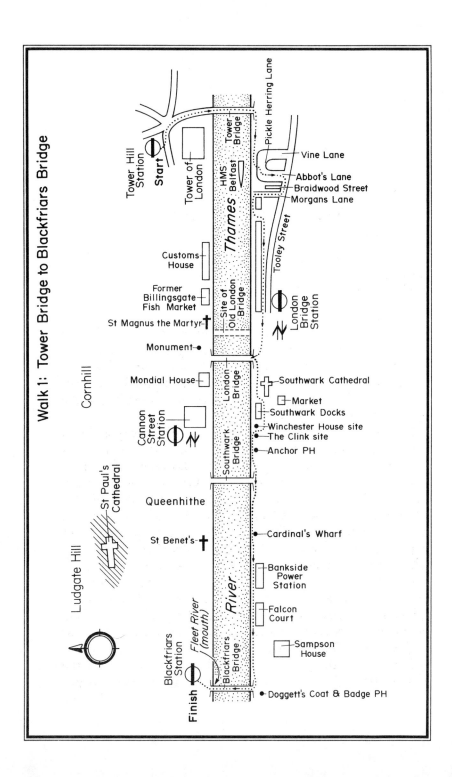

THE THAMES

1 Tower Bridge to Blackfriars Bridge
1¾ miles (2.8km)

Trains: Tower Hill underground station
Buses: 23, 42, 78
Map: OS Sheet no 177

Our subject is a tremendous one and starts where the old Roman and medieval city of London began with the eastern wall at the Tower of London. The famous 'mile' (later extended to the end of Fleet Street) ran west to the Fleet River (where Blackfriars Bridge now is) and from London Wall in the north to the River Thames.

It is not a long walk but it is packed with history and you may want to linger and ponder on the past. The walk traverses the exact length of the old City which today retains almost the same boundaries as in medieval times. As we walk we can recall the old Celtic encampments huddled on the few available dry sites; the stupendous Roman city (AD 43–410) of Londinium which replaced them; the subsequent medieval muddle of imposing church spires amid timber and thatch; or imagine the whole area consumed by the 'most horrid malicious bloody flame' (Pepys) of the Great Fire of 1666; we might hear the ghosts of those wailing the dead in the ceaseless plagues and epidemics of an overcrowded city or the laughter and shouting of our ancestors as they watched a bear being torn to shreds or Shakespeare's *The Comedy of Errors*.

Throughout the social saga ran the eternal waters of the Thames (though it used to freeze up and run almost dry!).

From coracle to long boat, man-of-war to stately East India-man, from the busy congestion of nineteenth-century lighters, coasters, wherries and barges to the quiet of today's occa-sional river bus or inflatable, the Thames remains uniquely fascinating.

We start on the south side of Tower Bridge, perhaps London's most famous landmark. It was opened in 1894 and replaced, as did all our bridges, long-established ferries. Many years were swallowed up in protracted negotiations to obtain land for approach roads (note the extent of the viaduct on the north side), in settling compensation for the ferrymen and get-ting a satisfactory design which would allow safe passage for tall-masted sailing ships to and from the Pool of London. The chosen design was submitted by Sir Horace Jones; it was at first shelved but later taken up again and completed after his death by Sir John Wolfe Barry. Sir Horace took every opportunity to incorporate steel and iron into the design and they form both a flowing and practical feature of the bridge (as also of his fine markets at Smithfield and Leadenhall). Originally the roadway in the form of two bascules would open twenty times a day for

Tower Bridge from Bermondsey

the passage of tall sailing ships so an overhead walkway was incorporated into the design to enable pedestrians to cross when the bridge was open; it was also a huge tie-beam and carried power to the north bascule. However, even before World War I, ships had mainly turned to steam and they could pass without the need to open the bascules. The walkway, rarely used, was therefore closed and remained so until 1982 when it was reopened as one of London's finest tourist sights. The old bascule-raising brass and copper steam engines were in use until 1976 (electric motors are now used for the rare openings) and the whole, together with the walkway and engine house, is now a museum. Take the stairs (south end) down to ground level and, with the river to your right, go west.

Look across to the Tower of London. This, the eastern extremity of the City of London, has been fortified since the Romans erected probably a wooden tower or look-out on this site. Some sort of structure existed when William I gained the English throne, but it was he who built the high central keep in 1078; the pretty caps on the corners are by Wren. The 'Conqueror' was a king of extraordinarily modern views on 'public relations' and 'image' for he built everywhere enormous keeps and castles of fine white Caen stone just to remind the unruly Saxons of his ubiquitous presence. However, the Tower has never had to withstand an invader. Its present form took about two hundred years to complete, encasing William's White Tower ever deeper behind layers of walls. Although it has never had to withstand an invader, it has acted variously as prison, palace and menagerie. It is now London's chief tourist attraction. Before the embankment of the Thames, the river flowed right up to the walls of the Tower, filling its moat and enabling boats to enter by the notorious Traitors' Gate. Incidentally, the Tower looked much bigger when it loomed directly over the water, as we can judge from old illustrations.

The two church spires opposite have a connection. The green copper tower of All Hallows-by-the-Tower is the site from which Samuel Pepys looked on the first morning of the Great Fire to see the devastation already caused across London; while the other spire, white and slender as a pencil, was the first designed by Wren after the Great Fire.

The path continues with a steady flow of visitors to HMS *Belfast*. The largest cruiser ever built for the Royal Navy, she is now a museum (*see* Walk 17). Although her presence here might at first seem incongruous, the clambering of small boys about her superstructure reflects the river's new role of recreation and leisure. However, the former commercial glories of the Pool of London (of which this is the Upper Pool) is still symbolically conveyed by the grand Egypto-Classical tower of the Port of London Authority (*see* Walk 17). You can see it to the left of the Tower of London and further back.

The route turns left shortly before reaching the HMS *Belfast* (though it will eventually carry on). It passes through an archway, winds right (Pickle Herring Street), then left between magnificent Victorian warehouses still used for storage. At Tooley Street turn right, then right again down Morgans Lane. Here you come to the Southwark Crown Court, an immense cube of honey-coloured brick, opened by Princess Anne in 1983. It is an imposing building in keeping with the intention of lining the river with architecture of merit. Continue on down to the spacious waterfront noting the high flood-barrier walls, then on round to the Victorian warehouses ahead.

This is Hay's Wharf, which takes its name from Alexander Hay who started the business in 1651. It remained with the family for nearly two hundred years so that when it passed to John Humphrey in 1838 the original name stuck. So, in fact, did the goods which it handled, and it continued as the company which dealt with most of the food imported into London. This wonderful range of industrial buildings has been one of the most hotly discussed sites in London. Racked by industrial disputes, it ceased as a mercantile industry in 1970 and although it still handles lorry-borne goods for storage this is an interim use before redevelopment. The principal buildings surrounding a small dock are now listed. They were built by William Cubitt in 1856 and have an outward simplicity and sense of security. Nothing could be more appropriate to its task nor more beautifully proportioned than the crane-bedecked dock enclosure. The huge iron gates to Tooley Street, also by Cubitt, complete the sense of purpose.

Continue along Tooley Street where the London home of

the Priors of Lewes used to stand, together with many other ecclesiastics' homes in this area. The range of river warehouses to your right was built in 1861 after the worst fire in London since 1666. The Great Fire of Tooley Street, like the Great Fire itself, began on a Saturday in summer. It started in a building stocked with hemp and jute, spread to others containing tallow and oil and another which exploded. In all, it burned for a fortnight and became London's principal attraction: there was a brisk trade in ginger beer and hot pies, the river was crowded with every imaginable sort of boat and sightseers brought traffic on nearby London Bridge to a stop. The fire-fighting system was so disorganised and ineffective that one positive outcome was the formation of the Metropolitan Fire Brigade.

The huge blocks to the left are Guy's Hospital but keep to the pavement until reaching the headquarters of the Hay's Wharf Company (bravely stated in immense gold letters). This fine building (Goodhart-Rendel 1931) is one of the most recent dates to be listed, its vigorous art-deco detailing and deliberate modernism now much admired. Note especially the black and gold heraldic main entrance through the covered courtyard. The river front of the building has an enormous central panel made up of bronze reliefs with copper columns below. On this site stood the church of St Olave until 1926 (there used to be four so named in London; now only St Olave, Hart Street, remains). Perhaps the old pronunciation was something like 'ooleeve' because Tooley is a corruption of St Olave. In 1008 he helped to expel the Danes by the extreme measure of destroying the wooden London Bridge. In those days its southern approach was just where the church was later built.

Return to Tooley Street and continue to the top of the bridge. Turn right onto London Bridge for a fine view of the Thames. The present bridge was opened in 1973. It was constructed using a brilliant technique of building above the previous bridge (thus maintaining traffic flow) which was sold, dismantled and re-erected as a tourist attraction at Lake Havasu Arizona, USA, the purchase price of £1,200,000 being recouped in a year or so. Although popular conception in the United States was that it was Tower Bridge which they were buying, they did, in fact, receive a superb work (1831) from the

15

great early nineteenth-century engineer John Rennie; we will shortly see the remaining southern arch of that bridge. Rennie's bridge replaced, in turn, the famous medieval bridge (1209) which, according to the old nursery rhyme, was always 'falling down'. The position of that bridge was slightly downstream; its southern approach was beside the white Hay's Wharf building and ran across to just behind the large Adelaide House at the north-east corner from where we stand. The old bridge was protected by a church at either end but only St Magnus the Martyr (Wren 1687) remains on the north side. Rennie, without modern building techniques to maintain traffic flow, had to build his bridge next to the old one which was then demolished. The bridge of 1209, however, was a comparative youngster beside the previous thousand-year-old wooden structure which was built by the Romans. In 1982–83 there were a hundred archaeologists from the Museum of London working here. They found amazing evidence of the Roman bridge, estimated to have been built about AD50, a Saxon quay nearby and foundations of St Botolph's Church (destroyed in the Great Fire) with medieval burials in the churchyard.

One might say that London began here. The Romans approached London via a spur of raised land, still discernible, that ran up through Southwark, continued through the bed of the river making it shallower at this point (it could almost dry out in a rainless summer) and on up to form Cornhill. It was an established crossing long before the Romans came and remained the only bridge in London until a similarly established site was chosen for Westminster Bridge some 1700 years later. The bridge of 1209 was the first stone bridge here (the first of three) and at 12ft (3.5m) wide was little more than a footbridge. The regulations which required Londoners to live within the city walls (Elizabeth I was particularly strict in its enforcement) compelled Londoners to use every available piece of space. This led to the building of houses upon the old bridge itself. They hung out perilously over each side of the bridge being propped up with wooden poles; not surprisingly, they were always 'falling down'. More distinguished were the Chapel of St Thomas à Becket at the bridge's centre and

Nonsuch House (amply describing itself) at the southern end. All this superstructure, however, was removed in George Dance's restoration of 1762.

Also behind Adelaide House lies Pudding Lane where, in 1666, began the Great Fire of London, to commemorate which Wren erected his towering 202ft (60.5m) column The Monument (you could make a short detour). The tragic story of this catastrophe of human wilfulness in ignoring long-standing fire regulations is best read in Pepys' account in his diary for September of 1666. The immensity of that drama is beyond the telling of this book but we should remember that from now until we reach Blackfriars Bridge, and slightly beyond, our every step will record the passage of the flames, 'one entire arch of fire above a mile long', fanned by a searing east wind.

The excellent buildings which can be seen from the bridge include (downstream north side) the Customs House (Smirke 1825), long, low Classical with trees fronting, and Billingsgate Market (Sir Horace Jones 1875), fish market until 1982 where so much of archaeological value was found on an adjacent site before development. Upstream on the south side can be seen the top of Southwark Cathedral and, by the bridge, the nice Victorian Hibernia Chambers (1850) which we cross over to and down the stairs to Montague Close. Here you can see the one remaining arch of Rennie's bridge. Continue west into the square.

Southwark Cathedral has been rather off the beaten track and less known than it should be. This is a fine example of the Early English style of architecture, with a sense of angular slenderness in the narrow lancet windows and profusion of thin columns, especially inside in the exquisite choir. Beginning as a Saxon nunnery in AD606, it was called St Mary Overie (ie over the rie or river) and was founded by the daughter of the local ferryman. It suffered during Henry VIII's Dissolution of the Monasteries and became the parish church of St Saviour, remaining so until 1905 when it became Southwark Cathedral. A great number of poets and actors, through the proximity of a number of theatres, were associated with the church; Shakespeare had a house close by the east end. Previously surrounded by the maze of alleys and warehouses (1858) of

St Paul's, set within a modern townscape

Southwark Docks, the cathedral now looks out onto a superb new piazza, Montague Close, with a fine view across the river. Fishmongers' Hall (Henry Roberts 1831) is directly opposite. To the left the white glass-fibre-clad Mondial House (Hubbard, Ford 1974) is an international telephone exchange. The twin black towers of Cannon Street Station (Hawkshaw 1866) make a wonderful contrast with the distant dome of St Paul's. This lovely piazza should develop into a splendid open-air space for recreation and the arts and bring due recognition to the cathedral.

Architecturally, the piazza is exactly to scale with the cathedral. It was created as part of the Queen Elizabeth Silver Jubilee Celebrations on a site given by the Hay's Wharf Company in 1977. The two new buildings on the east side are excellent but the new Grindley's Bank on the west side is superb (Michael Twigg 1983). Though undoubtedly modern in effect, this contains subtle references to traditional river architecture: the use of brick; rounded window arches at the bottom rather than at the top, their 'feet' jutting out overhead like hoisting gear; and the free, asymmetrical plan of a wharf-side range. The entrance is a huge Norman porch complete with a sloping ramp like a drawbridge. Following round, you come to the wonderful old St Mary's Dock narrowly hemmed in by a Victorian warehouse on the left and its modern equivalent on the right.

Opposite the west front of the cathedral is Southwark Market, its open-air pens of fruit and vegetables a nostalgic reminder of the old Covent Garden Market. Looking back at the cathedral from this point reveals perhaps its most attractive view. Continue to the T-junction; turn right and right again. Winchester Walk here recalls the London home of the Bishops of Winchester built in 1107. Its splendours can still be judged high up in the rose window of the ruins of the Great Hall. Here it was that in 1540 the middle-aged Henry VIII met teen-aged Catherine Howard.

Retrace your steps and continue ahead between tall warehouses. This is Clink Street where the Bishops of Winchester had a prison for religious heretics which gave a colloquial name for prisons throughout the English-speaking world. Three of those who suffered in 1593 had established an independent church in Southwark. This began the movement which eventually led the Pilgrim Fathers to leave the country for America in the Mayflower in 1620. Turn right at The Anchor, a really delightful pub, and on to the riverside.

Southwark was the scene of religious persecutions in the sixteenth and seventeenth centuries because of the number of ecclesiastics' homes in the area, including that of the Bishop of Rochester. Its near neighbour, Bankside, where we now stand, was, by contrast, the centre of entertainment and loose life since these activities were not allowed across the river in the City. Immorality was catered for in the splendidly named 'stews', saunas as we now call them, and in such immoral houses as Paris Garden which was leased from the Abbot of Bermondsey. Quite acceptable entertainment in those days was found at the various bear-baiting gardens (Elizabeth I was a keen spectator), but Bankside is best remembered for the glories of its Globe Theatre and the performances of Shakespeare and his contemporaries. Recent discoveries have located the exact site of the Globe and a replica is to be built. The view across the river is attractive with Alexandra Bridge

(1864) to the right and Southwark Bridge (Sir Ernest George 1921) to the left, the latter in antique style to harmonise with Blackfriars Bridge further down and, indeed, the City itself of those days. Continue on to Southwark Bridge and wind round through the arch to the river again.

Here there are steps down to the water; at low tide you can see a cobbled slipway. All along the river there are fascinating accesses to and from the water now rarely used. A hundred yards further on you will see, on the north bank, Bull's Wharf and next to it the small inlet known as Queenhithe. Bull's Wharf has recently been rebuilt; and it is good to see its traditional style and its height kept relative to St Paul's. Since the ninth century ships have docked at Queenhithe; Billingsgate and Queenhithe were the two principal ports in London. Originally it was Quern Hithe or even Corn Hithe after the corn that was landed and milled at the quern. However, Queen Eleanor (1246–90) received revenue from goods landed at the port so that its name seems to have had several origins. Always a flourishing commercial area, the Hansa merchants had their warehouses here from 1157, and the Vintry of the wine trade; Vintners' Hall (1671) is still here. Both Chaucer and Dick Whittington had houses at Queenhithe.

Further along we come to the cobbled area of Cardinal's Wharf (probably named after Cardinal Wolsey) and the little house, with commemorative plaque, where Christopher Wren lived while St Paul's Cathedral was being built. Here also Catherine of Aragon spent her first night in London in 1502. Looking across to St Paul's, one can see how well Wren chose where to live. In those days the houses surrounding the church would have been tiny by comparison so he could have seen virtually the entire side elevation. Crossing the river he would have landed at Paul's Wharf and, passing his own delightful little red-brick church of St Benet's, seen just above the north bank, would have climbed up Ludgate Hill.

Next we come to a modern industrial masterpiece, Bankside Power Station by Sir Giles Gilbert Scott. Not completed until 1952, it had only thirty years of full service before its closure in 1982. Scott's other great Thameside power station at Battersea (closed 1983) has now been listed but Bankside is causing more debate. Ironically, it may have been Scott's expertise in channelling all outlets into one huge central chimney (Battersea has four) which, with the long low line of the building, gives it a somewhat bleak outline when seen from the other side of the river, but from our view it looks superb, with fine brick detailing, rather Egyptian in style.

The view across the river again is splendid. A stainless-steel panorama lists what you can see which includes, apart from the National Westminster Tower (Seifert 1979), no fewer than ten of Wren's churches. The whole of the Bankside river walk is a delight. In front of the power station and the attractive Falcon Court housing estate the river wall has been well built up. Another impressive modern building is next to Blackfriars Bridge. Sampson House (Fitzroy Robinson 1978) is Lloyd's Bank computer centre. At a distance, the concrete walls look as bright as aluminium, and the building has an engaging, intricate quality.

Passing under the arch we arrive at the top of the stairs between two bridges; if the tide is out there is a great view from the strand under the arches to the City. Actually there are three bridges here: Blackfriars and the two railway bridges. The main road bridge is by Joseph Cubitt (1869), and is notable for its massive polished granite columns with elaborate capitals surmounted by pulpits. These are fine viewing points. In the centre of the road crossing the bridge there is the dragon and arms of the City of London, the precincts of which we now enter – unless, that is, you wish to show your appreciation of a slice of waterway history at the Doggett's Coat and Badge pub just opposite. This is named after a famous race for licensed rivermen in which the winner is awarded a colourful coat and badge. Cross the bridge to Blackfriars station but on the way look across to the cluster of trees of Inner and Middle Temple to your left. It was not until this point was reached that the Great Fire finally burnt out.

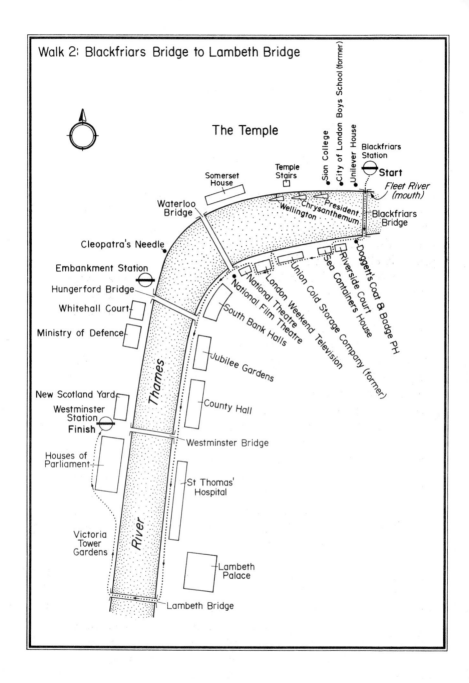

Walk 2: Blackfriars Bridge to Lambeth Bridge

The Temple

Sion College

City of London Boys School (former)

Unilever House

Blackfriars Station

Start

Somerset House

Temple Stairs

Fleet River (mouth)

Wellington

Chrysanthemum

President

Blackfriars Bridge

Waterloo Bridge

Cleopatra's Needle

Riverside Court

Doggett's Coat & Badge PH

Embankment Station

Hungerford Bridge

Whitehall Court

Ministry of Defence

National Theatre

London Weekend Television

National Film Theatre

South Bank Halls

Union Cold Storage Company (former)

Sea Containers House

Thames

Jubilee Gardens

New Scotland Yard

Westminster Station

Finish

County Hall

Houses of Parliament

Westminster Bridge

St Thomas' Hospital

Victoria Tower Gardens

River

Lambeth Palace

Lambeth Bridge

2   Blackfriars Bridge to Lambeth Bridge
2 miles (3.2km)

Trains: Blackfriars (underground and British Rail)
Buses: 45, 63, 70
Map: OS Sheet no 177

The great word hereabouts is Fleet. Fleet Street, Fleet River, Fleet Prison and Fleet Weddings. The weddings were performed by clerical malefactors who could purchase time off from the prison to marry couples on the spot for a fee. It became a fashionable prank in the eighteenth century to get married in this way but the practice was stopped in 1753 and the prison itself was demolished in 1844.

The word 'fleet' has an Anglo-Saxon origin meaning a navigable river as opposed to a brook or a stream. Regrettably we cannot walk the course of the River Fleet as it was arched over and covered in stages between 1733 and 1766. However, we can still see its sources in the ponds at Highgate (in the grounds of Kenwood House) and at Hampstead. Rivulets flowing from the ponds joined together at Camden Town, flowed through Holborn (the 'bourne in the hollow') and assumed a grand scale down the line of Farringdon Street under which it still runs. If you look under the north arch of Blackfriars Bridge at low tide you will see the mouth of the once navigable Fleet. It was expected that the Great Fire would be stopped by the river, but the flames leapt straight across it and carried on. So much rubble fell in, and indeed was thrown in, that it never really recovered. A Roman barge loaded with stone, presumably intended for building London's wall, was found deep in the mud near the mouth of the Fleet in 1962. It is now in the Museum of London.

At the junction of two rivers one can expect to find much of interest: the east side of Farringdon Street was the site of the western part of London's medieval wall; there was a flourishing market until 1830; the Dominican monks, or Blackfriars, had their monastery here until 1538; there were three theatres, the Duke, Salisbury and the Playhouse (which used the refectory of the former monastery); Ben Jonson, Shakespeare and

23

Van Dyck lived nearby; the miraculous Bride's Well was a place of pilgrimage; and Henry VIII had his Bridewell Palace (1520) which later became an infamous prison until transferred to Holloway in 1855. Still with us is the lovely church of St Bride's (Wren 1678, spire 1703). Its 'wedding-cake' spire did, in fact, give the idea of a tiered cake to a baker who could see it from his premises on Ludgate Hill. It is the highest of Wren's spires and quite the best known.

From Blackfriars station turn left and go over the bridge. Go down the stairs beside Doggett's Coat and Badge pub onto the riverside walk. Across the river can be seen the huge white curve of Unilever House (1931), on the site of Bridewell, with its enormous sculptures by Sir William Reid Dick; then the 1880s 'Renaissance' of the former City of London Boys' School and next to it the red brick Victorian Gothic of Sion College (Blomfield 1886) which houses the theological library of the Church of England (open to the public).

On our side we have the attractive Riverside Court (Seifert 1977) bringing residential use back to the riverside. Next is the big Sea Containers House (Seifert 1977). Take the narrow passage to the main street (Upper Ground) and turn right. The setting is now theatrically modernistic: an overhead walkway, the massive King's Reach Tower (IPC Magazines) and varied shapes of buildings closely spaced in a free arrangement. We proceed rather awe-struck until we reach the splendid sweep of Stamford Wharf of the former Union Cold Storage Company.

This wonderful range is now listed. Its famous Oxo Tower is a good art-deco landmark which was hotly campaigned for; supporters stood on Blackfriars Bridge collecting signatures in 1983. Follow along the building's curve and go down the narrow Barge House Alley which is off to the right. At the end there are steps going up and then down again (flood barrier) to a long landing place, a helicopter pad for courier services and, at low tide, London's finest river foreshore: it is worth trying to make it at that time.

Walking along the shore you see the river front of what was Europe's largest meat storage plant: the sombre facade, the great loading bay with lighting for night-time work, the cranes and the old lettering reminiscent of work that stopped in 1974.

At one time the rising tide would fill vast tanks below the warehouses, the water being released at low tide in a mighty surge to cleanse the foreshore; you can still see the pipes. Disputes with the rivermen led to closure of this enormous site overnight. An argument against the retention of some of the river warehouses was that they broke the line of the planned riverside walk.

Look down under Blackfriars Bridge to the City: we do not often see the City from this lowly position. On the north bank opposite, permanently moored, from right to left, are HMS *President* and HMS *Chrysanthemum* (Royal Naval Reserve) and HQS *Wellington* (Worshipful Company of Mariners). Between the last two can be seen Sir Joseph Bazalgette's impressive Temple Stairs (1868). This marks the present western limit of the City of London.

Return to the street and turn right. The enormous building on the right is London Weekend Television (Elson, Pack and Roberts 1971) shimmering in white mosaic. More exciting though is IBM's Kingdom House (Lasdun 1983) and the National Theatre (Lasdun 1976), its piled up boxes suggesting the enclosed audience chambers within. The idea of a National Theatre was first proposed in 1848, and strenuous efforts for its realisation were maintained from the turn of this century. Matters had got as far as the laying of foundation stones at four different sites before Princess Elizabeth, as she then was, finalised the present site in 1951. Denys Lasdun was appointed architect in 1949, nearly thirty years before the building was completed, and it contains three auditoriums of 400, 890 and 1160 capacity. At night it is illuminated, the concrete surfaces dissolving into areas of light-sculpture. By taking the service road beside the theatre we come to the Riverside Walk which will take us all the way to Lambeth Bridge. The views from here are splendid with Somerset House (opposite) and Waterloo Bridge.

Somerset House (Sir William Chambers 1786) originally had the waters of the Thames lapping right up to its walls. The black recesses of the arches were actually water gates. Its dignified Palladianism makes it one of London's greatest Classical buildings, though it has lost some of its height through the Embankment. The original building (1550) was built for Lord Protector Somerset. It was demolished in 1775. The present building took some sixty years (1776–1835) before it reached its present state. It was built as government offices and as the home of artistic and learned societies, the Royal Society, the Royal Academy of Arts and the Society of Antiquaries. At one time the Navy also occupied part of the building, and Nelson frequently attended meetings there.

Waterloo Bridge (Sir Giles Gilbert Scott 1945), though undeniably modern, possesses the same Classical restraint and rhythmic elegance as Somerset House. The bridge is by far the most elegant in London which is fortunate as it replaced John Rennie's masterpiece (1817) which was described by the great Italian sculptor Canova as 'the noblest bridge in the world'. Scott's bridge has two subtle features in its design. First, it is the only one which begins not at the water's edge but crosses it on both sides to encompass a road on the north and the Riverside Walk on the south. Secondly, this elongation is made to appear even more slender by the darker-toned material used to frame the arches which concentrates the eye upon the white areas. Originally called Strand Bridge, the name 'Waterloo' was brought in because Rennie's great design was thought to be an appropriate tribute to the Duke of Wellington after his famous victory at the Battle of Waterloo.

The lamp standards along this walk are almost identical to the famous 'Dolphin' standards (Vulliamy 1870) on the north bank. They are all cast from the same mould but with the difference that these on the south bank have substituted the date 1964 and EIIR (Elizabeth Regina II) for VR (Victoria Regina). Further along there are others dated 1910 (Edward VII) and 1933 (George V).

Passing under the south arch of Waterloo Bridge, the National Film Theatre must have the most unusual site of any cinema in the country; it lies under the approach road to the bridge. It began as part of the Festival of Britain (1951) but proved to be so successful that it has continued ever since.

Here the Thames turns an exact right angle from the east–west line we have been taking to a near-perfect north–south; it is a spectacular sweep. The world of entertainment continues to be represented with three concert halls: Queen Elizabeth Hall and the Purcell Room together (1967) and then the Royal Festival Hall (Matthew and Martin 1951). This was a milestone in London's architectural history for it was the first important public building in the contemporary style, though it was a couple of decades later than continental developments. It is still refreshing, cheerful and gentle today. Even if music is not your subject there are restaurants and bars that can be visited. It has the extraordinary virtues of being at once complex and varied and yet the easiest of places to find your way around. The only surviving structure from the Festival of Britain (1951) its name is still apposite for the youngsters of today, for it is a truly 'festive' hall.

Across the river is Victoria Embankment Gardens, with exceptionally pretty curving pathways, and Cleopatra's Needle seemingly jutting out of the water. It is actually about fourteen hundred years older than Cleopatra. It was erected in about 1475BC but Cleopatra's name was added to it very much later. It was a gift to this country in 1819, from Mohammed Ali, Turkish Viceroy of Egypt, after its loss at sea and the attendant deaths of six sailors, before it was placed on the Embankment 'adorning nothing, emphasising nothing, and by nothing emphasised' as was solemnly written in *The Builder* at the time.

Behind the gardens rises a quite popular work. Shell-Mex House is like a titanic mantlepiece clock. What we can see is the 1931 facade designed by Joseph's (architects) which was placed onto the old Cecil Hotel; in its day the largest hotel in Europe. To the right is the world-famous Savoy Hotel (Collcutt 1889) on the site of John of Gaunt's stupendous Savoy Palace which was destroyed in Wat Tyler's Peasants' Revolt of 1381. The hotel, commissioned by D'Oyly Carte (manager of the Gilbert and Sullivan 'Savoy' operettas) is a subtly refined building faced in cream terracotta Doulton tiles. When it opened it was distinguished by its great number of bathrooms and its electric lights and lifts. Ritz and Escoffier's personal records of clients' tastes and excentricities amount to an extraordinary social study.

Continue under Hungerford Bridge which looks better from the south-west side. The first bridge was a very elegant footbridge (1836) built by the great Isambard Kingdom Brunel. It led to the popular Hungerford Market. When the market was replaced by Charing Cross station in 1863 its engineer, John Hawkshaw, also built the iron railway bridge but had to incorporate a footbridge to maintain a right of way; it is still there today. The iron chains of Brunel's suspension bridge were not wasted; they can be seen on Clifton Suspension Bridge which he built at Bristol.

Across the river is the fairytale skyline of Whitehall Court (Archer and Green 1884) and the National Liberal Club (Waterhouse 1887). With a fine sunset behind it, it is London's most startling silhouette; a French chateau fantasy. To the left is the bleak, blank Ministry of Defence. It was built in 1959 to a design by Vincent Harris which was already forty-six years old and which had won the competition but had been delayed by two world wars and was then just forgotten about. The announcement of another competition eventually brought the earlier winner out of retirement, plans under his arm, to the amazement of everybody. But in spite of the wonderful site this 'monument of tiredness', as Pevsner calls it, went ahead and was built.

Behind us is Jubilee Gardens so named in 1977 to celebrate the Silver Jubilee of Queen Elizabeth II. The towering Shell Centre (Easton 1963) was an early part of the South Bank's development. At the foot of its walls Australians have established a zany tradition by lining the roads with their caravanettes which they want to sell before returning home. Then comes County Hall (Ralph Knott 1908–22), a late example of Edwardian Italian Renaissance . It was built by the old London County Council, which moved from its former premises in Spring Gardens near Trafalgar Square, and was subsequently occupied by the Greater London Council. Together with additional blocks, it was not completed until 1963. Some of the fine marble interiors can be seen in the corridors and Council Chamber. A Roman boat, now in the Museum of London, which was found in 1910 during excavating for the foundations for County Hall, indicates the fact that the Thames was much wider before the embankments were built.

Directly opposite is New Scotland Yard which, until 1967,

was the famous Metropolitan Police Headquarters (Norman Shaw 1890 and 1906). The medieval Scotland Yard (for the reception of Scottish kings) lay behind Whitehall Court and there, in 1829, the police established their first headquarters. When they moved to Westminster Bridge they took the name with them adding 'New' to the title. In 1967 the headquarters of the Metropolitan Police was moved to Victoria Street and this, their former home, was renamed Norman Shaw Building.

At this point the view across the river is one of the greatest in the land; Westminster Bridge to the Houses of Parliament represents the pinnacle of English design when we led the world in a revival of the Gothic style. The first bridge here (1750) was only the second to be built in London since the Romans began London Bridge. Planning included lengthy negotiations over compensation to ferrymen. The Archbishop of Canterbury received payments for the loss of his horse ferry (Horseferry Road still exists) almost equal to the combined total received by all the watermen concerned. The present bridge is cast-iron and was completed to the design of Thomas Page in 1862. It is full of rich detail especially in the fine lamp clusters. To the left as you reach the bridge note the magnificent lion. It was made in 1837 from the superb substance known as Coade Stone. The secret formula for its composition was undisclosed when the proprietor of the firm, Mrs Eleanor Coade, died in 1840. The lion, made originally for the Lion Brewery at Hungerford Bridge, now marks the site of the Coade factory.

Keeping to the south bank, cross the bridge and enter Albert Embankment (Bazalgette 1870) which runs in front of St Thomas' Hospital (Henry Currey 1871). The hospital was founded about 1106 and was attached to what is now Southwark Cathedral. It was dedicated to St Thomas à Becket about seventy years later. A hundred years ago this hospital embodied the most advanced practice of preventing the spread of disease: blocks separated by low corridors according to the principles of Florence Nightingale. At the far end is the delightful Medical School with its Italianate chimney.

The Houses of Parliament (more correctly Westminster Palace) are situated on a straight section of Lambeth Reach which they share with Victoria Tower Gardens. They occupy a site which has been that of a royal palace (hence their official name) and our government for a thousand years. Not surprisingly we can see the swings of political and cultural fashion embodied in the present building. It has been called a masterpiece of compromise. A Classical plan with Victorian Gothic detail, it was completed in 1852 after a fire (1834) had destroyed the elegant but impractical government buildings of Sir John Soane. Charles Barry, who won the competition for a Gothic design, was practical above all things. His design won partly because it was excellently thought out with regard to the movements of MPs but also because of the exquisite drawings which were submitted; Barry had engaged the incredible young virtuoso of the drawing-board, Augustus Pugin, to design the Gothic detail. For many years it was the most astounding administrative building in the world. And an influential one too, for it positively established the growing interest in reviving Gothic design.

Albert Embankment is for pedestrians only and is a quiet

Lambeth Palace

walk with a mood of historic dignity. Lambeth Reach is calming in the directness of its line yet it was across this stretch of water that the Gunpowder Plot conspirators (1605) crossed by water from their rented house on the south bank. At the end of St Thomas's we meet the garden wall and imposing gatehouse of Lambeth Palace, which has been the London home of the Archbishop of Canterbury for nearly eight hundred years. The earliest parts of this endearing scattered residence date from the thirteenth century (the crypt under the chapel) but it is the red-brick gatehouse of the main entrance which has supreme excellence. Built by Archbishop Morton at the end of the fifteenth century, it is one of the finest Tudor buildings in London and must be compared with the gatehouse of St James's Palace.

The river used to come right up to the palace wall behind which lies London's next largest private garden after that of Buckingham Palace. The nearby church was the former parish church of St Mary. It is now a garden centre named after John Tradescant (after whom tradescantia is called) who was buried here, as was Admiral Bligh of HMS *Bounty* and several Archbishops of Canterbury.

Go over Lambeth Bridge to the north side. The first bridge here was built in 1861. The present one is by Blomfield and Topham Forrest (1932) and is a delightful example of the historic style — meaning that it looks older than it is. Splendid obelisks stand at each entrance; there are attractive iron and stone lamp-standards and it has unusually high arching towards the centre to allow safe passage for shipping. Views from the bridge are lovely; Lambeth Palace looks at its best from here.

Immediately after crossing the bridge, turn right down the steps into Victoria Tower Gardens named after the huge tower which is seen ahead. Continue with the river to your right. In the gardens you can see the jolly little Victorian Gothic Buxton Memorial Fountain (Teulon 1865) erected to the memory of the leader of the Anti-Slavery Party, Sir Thomas Buxton. The eight small statues of British rulers around the cornice are made of fibreglass, the original bronze ones having been stolen in 1960 when the fountain was moved from Parliament Square to the comparative seclusion of these gardens. There is also a statue of Mrs Pankhurst (Walker 1928) and a copy of Rodin's deeply moving and justly famous 'Bergers of Calais' (1895).

The path leads out of the gardens, so continue past the Houses of Parliament (Westminster Palace) for buses and Westminster underground station.

3 Chelsea Embankment
3 miles (4.8km) (circular walk)

Trains: Sloane Square underground station
Buses: 11, 137
Map: OS Sheet no 176

From Sloane Square underground station go straight ahead out of the main exit and over the pedestrian crossing. Take the first left, Lower Sloane Street, and continue along Chelsea Bridge Road until you reach the Thames at Chelsea Embankment. Start at the corner of Chelsea Bridge Road and Chelsea Embankment. Walk beside the river with the river on your left. Chelsea Reach is straight for a mile long. With parks on both sides and the grand design of the embankment, this is the most eloquent section of the river in town. When they were riverside villages, Chelsea and Battersea faced each other across the water. Without the embankments the river would have been much wider, slower flowing and with broad edgings of river mud and gravel just beneath our present path. This idyllic rural scene was chosen in 1682 by Charles II for the quiet grandeur of his Royal Military Hospital to our right. Now called the Royal Hospital Chelsea, the Chelsea Flower Show is held in its grounds each year. Wren was the architect, though Adam and Soane completed the work over a period of about a hundred years.

Wren's design is low and calm with a minimum of decoration apart from the central portico. The low colonnade is a nice touch supplying a covered walkway for a damp climate. If you have allowed sufficient time, do go in and see the Chapel with its fine wood carving and the Great Hall where Wellington was laid in state in 1852. The thickly wooded park to the right of the hospital is Ranelagh Gardens, one of London's loveliest corners. From 1742 to 1804 it was the most refined of London's several pleasure gardens (Vauxhall, not far away, was another) where fashionable society met at concerts and grand balls. Ranelagh Gardens is delightfully laid out with winding paths which make a natural and informal route among a wealth of trees of special interest. Across the river, Battersea

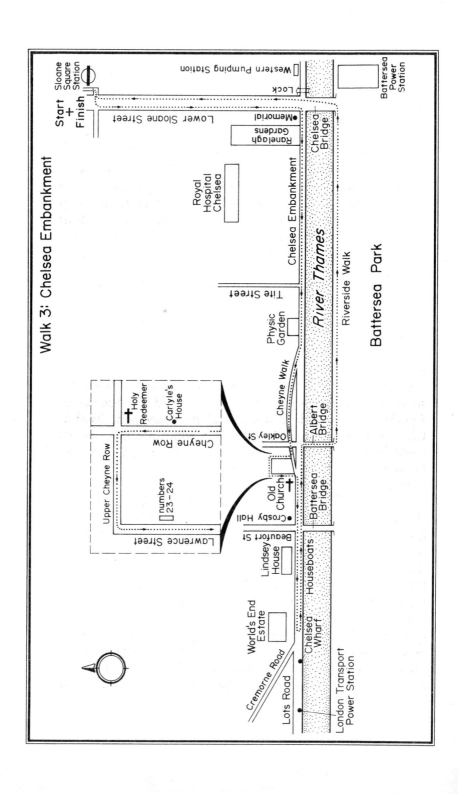

Walk 3: Chelsea Embankment

Park revived the local association with pleasure gardens in 1951 when its Fun Fair was opened as part of the Festival of Britain. More about the park later on.

The Royal Military Hospital began the break up of Chelsea's line of riverside cottages but it was the building of Bazalgette's Chelsea Embankment in 1871–74 which gave rise to the truly spectacular houses which follow. Beginning at No 1 Chelsea Embankment, they were all built in the 1870s to 80s and were studies, some of them quite brilliant, in adaptations of the Tudor, Renaissance and Queen Anne styles. A short detour up Tite Street takes us to a number of massive studio-homes built for leading artists of the time: Whistler at No 35, Sargent at No 31 and Oscar Wilde at No 64. Returning to the embankment No 8 (Clock House) and No 17 (Swan House) are the finest among an excellent group and were designed by Norman Shaw in about 1875. Clock House has a large eighteenth-century type clock and a virtuoso collection of window styles, while Swan House has a graceful and inventive use of ancient features, such as the two overhanging storeys, in a modern arrangement.

Continue along to the Chelsea Physic Garden, a delightful survival of ancient scientific study. In 1673 the Society of Apothecaries leased land from Sir Hans Sloane (who lived in Cheyne Walk) to establish a garden in which medicinal plants could be grown and researched. In 1722, being a naturalist himself, Sloane made the Society the gift of the ground 'in perpetuity' and its work continues today.

At the next road turn into Cheyne Walk, rich in architectural charm and artistic associations. Mostly early Georgian, each house has a style of its own but continuity is maintained by the outstanding wrought-iron railings and gates which are among the finest in London. In No 4 George Eliot died after only three weeks' occupation but No 16 has firmer literary associations with Rosetti, Swinburne and Meredith. Known as Queen's House it is the largest in the group and is in its original 1717 state, except for the out-of-character bay window. Go down the alley beside No 23 where 'drivers are requested to lead their horses'. Here stood Henry VIII's Manor House till 1753 when its last occupant, Sir Hans Sloane, died at the age of ninety-three. Some mulberry trees, allegedly planted by Elizabeth I, can still be seen at the far end of the lane. Cross Oakley Street and continue along the western section of Cheyne Walk. Many of the houses here are more typical of Chelsea before it became fashionable, some dating from about 1711.

In the small Embankment Gardens is the statue of Carlyle (Boehm 1882) which commemorates his residence at No 24 Cheyne Row for forty-seven years. Go up Cheyne Row which originated in Queen Anne's days; keeping to the left side affords the better view. Carlyle's house is maintained by the National Trust and is in a remarkably original state. The Church of The Holy Redeemer (Goldie 1895) stands on the site of de Morgan's Chelsea Pottery. Turn left (Upper Cheyne Row) for charming little cottages of about 1716, smaller and cheaper being further from the river, and into Lawrence Street, an exquisite setpiece. Chelsea porcelain was made here and Smollett and Fielding had their homes, the latter's, Nos 23–24, being amongst the finest of Chelsea's houses. This now brings us back to Cheyne Walk and Chelsea Old Church which was closely associated with Sir Thomas More whose statue we pass. Chelsea Old Church was the centre of the riverside village. It was almost entirely rebuilt (Walter Godfrey 1958) after receiving a direct hit on 16 April 1941. Extraordinarily, the very next day after that bomb fell, a parachute mine utterly obliterated the village cottages not 50yd (45m) away, where there is now a sunken garden, and thus removed the heart of the old village.

Cross through the sunken garden. In Danvers Street you can see the back of the fifteenth-century Crosby Hall; continue to the gate which leads to the front of the hall. It was built about 1475 in Bishopsgate for a City merchant but when threatened with demolition in 1910 it was re-erected here. It had survived the Great Fire and is a rare indication of the grand scale of living of the successful merchant of medieval times. Cross Beaufort Street (named after Sir Thomas More's Beaufort House) and take the riverside path to Lindsey House, last of the great Chelsea mansions. It was built in 1674 on the site of More's farm. It became the centre of the Moravian Brotherhood in 1752, when it received its Mansard roof, and was subdivided into the present seven houses in 1775. Whistler lived at No 96 and the great nineteenth-century engineers the Brunels, father and son, at No 98. Further along, Walter Greaves and Hillaire Belloc lived at No 103, Wilson Steer at No 108 (his studio at the top) and Turner at Nos 118–19 (bombed and restored), where he died. The skyscraper blocks of the World's End Estate (Cadbury Brown 1977) destroyed an old part of Chelsea which had been called World's End.

On the riverside is a once-celebrated houseboat community. In the 1950s and 1960s it was a brave and rebellious post-war venture. Now these quirky craft are done up as serious investments like everthing else, but there is still some fun. The tall white building to your right, Chelsea Wharf, is an excellent example of revived old warehouse buildings and was converted in 1979. With its central courtyard and invigorating waterside position, this collection of businesses and craftsmen has become a thriving community. Beyond Chelsea Wharf is the famous Lots Road Power Station, the electricity generating station for London Underground, and the Chelsea Creek, no longer busy commercially. An attempt was made to keep the creek for historic and recreational reasons but inexorably it was filled in and now only a short section of the mouth of the creek exists.

Return along the riverwalk to Albert Bridge but stop half-way along and compare it to Battersea Bridge. Prince Albert died in 1861 from typhoid, a virulent killer in the London of those days, and the following decades produced some remarkable works dedicated to his memory. The bridge, designed by R.M. Ordish and opened in 1873, has received its share of criticism along with other Albert memorials. Pevsner has called it prolix and Nairn describes it as 'a recognition of frailty and absurdity' but at a time when its suitability for modern traffic brought it close to demolition he went on to say 'No replacement will do'. Battersea Bridge was more celebrated when it was a wooden footbridge, which was demolished in the 1890s. It was the subject of a remarkably atmospheric painting by Whistler, a devoted artist of the Thames, which was called 'Nocturne'.

Continue to Albert Bridge, keep to the footpath under the

bridge and then cross over on the downstream side to Battersea Park. Entry is by a small gate immediately you reach the other side. The park is man-made and in a sense it took some three hundred years, on and off, to do it. It was in the sixteenth century that the marshy lands of Battersea Fields were first reclaimed and used for market gardening. Later on pigeon shooting, fairs, donkey racing and other diversions became popular so that the Festival Pleasure Gardens of 1951 had a precedent. In the nineteenth century 320 acres were drained and the ground level raised with earth excavated during the building of the Royal Victoria Docks in the 1850s. If the origins of this picturesque park seem rather mundane, we can recall the dashing event of Wellington v. Winchelsea in one of the last duels to be fought in England in 1829.

Our path takes us along the riverside again; a bracing walk after the richly historical north bank. We pass the old pier where visitors to the Festival Gardens would arrive by boat. Towards the end of this ¾ mile (1.2km) walk we have an amazing vision as the white chimneys of Battersea Power Station creep through the trees towards us, a very exciting view. This great cathedral of power was designed by the architect of Liverpool Cathedral, Sir Giles Gilbert Scott. It was

Battersea Power Station

not completed until the 1950s and was closed down early in 1983, the guided tours through spacious turbine halls and Stygian boiler rooms ceasing soon afterwards. The first turbine hall was completed in the 1930s and had walls hung with coloured glazed earthenware tiles. It was the most unusual building to be listed for preservation by the Department of the Environment and exciting plans were being considered for its future. Sports centre, giant discotheque, engineering museum, marina – all had been suggested and it was big enough to take them all. Pevsner describes it as 'one of the first examples in England of frankly contemporary industrial architecture'. In 1984 it was finally decided to develop it as a vast entertainment centre to stand comparison with the Tivoli gardens in Copenhagen and Disneyland in Los Angeles.

Cross over Chelsea Bridge which has tall lamp brackets each crowned with a golden galleon. A more efficient construction than Albert Bridge, no doubt, and generally admired ('concise, crisp, and spare', says Pevsner) but surely not so disarming as that latter ode to string and sealing-wax. Chelsea Bridge, designed by Topham Forrest, was opened in 1937 by the Prime Minister of Canada. The construction was by Rendel, Palmer and Tritton, the same firm which, fifty years later, constructed the great Woolwich Flood Barrier (1984) on the Thames.

The view upstream is the most tree-lined reach on London's Thames, the elegant Chelsea Embankment neatly picked out by the white orbs of the lamps. Just to the right can be seen the chimney of the Western Pumping Station, a grand Victorian industrial building built (1875) on the Grosvenor Estate. Consisting of property in Mayfair, Belgravia and Pimlico, the estate has been with the Grosvenor family (Dukes of Westminster since 1874) for over three hundred years and much of the immense revenue has always been put back into good-quality building. Mayfair's eighteenth-century terraces, Belgravia's early nineteenth-century squares and Pimlico's great Victorian churches are among the main achievements. To the left of the pumping station can be seen all that remains of the old Grosvenor Canal: the lock gates.

Continue straight ahead, past the Carabiniers Memorial and alongside Ranelagh Gardens back to Sloane Square. The memorial is to the officers and men of the regiment who fell in the Boer War (1899–1902) and was designed by Adrian Jones; his immense statue of Peace driving a four-horse chariot stands on top of the Constitution Arch at Hyde Park Corner.

One final thought. If you have followed this walk during the daytime, do consider walking the final section – the two bridges and Battersea Park riverwalk – at dusk. It is very romantic. The whole stretch is delightfully illuminated and it would be the perfect prelude to dinner in a Chelsea restaurant.

4   Dockland in the Pool of London
2¾ miles (4.5km) (circular walk)

Trains: Tower Hill underground station
Buses: 23, 42, 78
Map: OS sheet no 177

This walk smacks of the sea. If you go without wearing your
nautical kit you will find that others are wearing theirs. They
will probably not be authentic old salts, but rather those enthusiasts who like to mess around in boats. Without doubt,
however, we can count ourselves privileged to do this walk.
Last century we would have stood a good chance of having our
throats cut or of contracting a contagion before completing the
journey.

Turn left out of Tower Hill station, cross the open space and
head for the pedestrian subway, but have a look at the section
of old wall (left) before descending. It is London's finest remains of the ancient defence wall: Roman foundations and
medieval upper part. Go down the subway (toilets right) and
take the left fork going parallel to the Tower of London. The
green lawns are where the old moat used to be, filled by water
from the Thames. Continue under the archway, the road overhead, and take the stairs (left) to the street, turning sharp right
at the top – double-back in fact.

This is the celebrated – or infamous – Ratcliff Highway, formerly the most violent and murderous region in London; yet it
was within easy distance of elegant squares and terraces occupied by distinguished sea captains. On the right we come to a
large gate, with elephants on top of the piers, and we enter St
Katharine's Docks, where ivory was a valuable import. The
old cobbled road is beneath our feet, chandlers' shops are to the
left and right and, ahead, the refurbished warehouses stand on
a peninsula between docks on either side. Pass around to the
right of Ivory House and make for the archway which is ahead,
with a fine clocktower above.

The architects were Thomas Telford and Philip Hardwick
and their work represents the supreme achievement in London's dockland architecture. The docks were built between

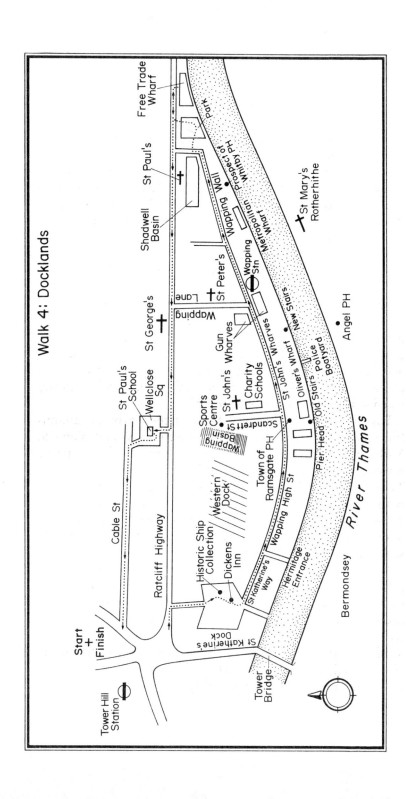

Walk 4: Docklands

1825 and 1828 against fierce opposition; more than 1,200 households were made homeless, without compensation and with no alternative accommodation. The families stayed in the area merely adding to the overcrowding. The old hospital of St Katharine's by the Tower, founded in 1148, was moved away from the smoke and noise and settled elegantly into a new home in Regent's Park.

Out of the archway, turn left, cross the retractable bridge and pass in front of the Dickens Inn (the Historic Ship Collection behind the inn is dealt with in Walk 17). The existence of the inn came about through the imaginative development of a piece of good luck. In 1972 while a nineteenth-century brewery warehouse was being demolished at St Katharine's the timber frame of an older building was discovered underneath bricks that were being removed. Closer examination revealed an eighteenth-century cladding. The excrescence was cleaned off and the old frame was moved on rollers, lock stock and barrel, 100yd (90m) to its present site. Some of the old bricks were re-used to form a base, their worn fronts reversed inwards, and the present delightful building emerged after a century in the dark. It was re-opened in 1976 and is already listed – that must be a world record!

Passing in front of the inn go between the two black columns (they all came from demolished warehouses) and along St Katharine's Way where we meet the first of the Wapping warehouses: British and Foreign Wharf. Pass the junction with Thomas Moore Street (left) and the dock entrance building with its medallion inscribed Port of London Authority 1914. Behind the huge walls (left) there used to be the Western Dock of the London Docks (1805–1969) but it has now been filled in and awaits building development.

London Docks were of particularly handsome design (Daniel Alexander) and contained extensive underground wine vaults linked by tunnels, all intended to combat theft. The surrounding walls were notable bastions. In all, the project consisted of the Western and Eastern Docks, the New Basin at Shadwell and several smaller basins. Crossing over the former Hermitage Entrance to the Western Docks (look over the low wall to the right), we enter Wapping High Street.

Wapping was developed in the latter part of the sixteenth century in the hope that residents would drain the area and build up a wall against the frequent floodings; it received its own parish church (St John's) in 1617. But development was slow. Even in 1625 it was still possible for Charles I to kill a stag which he pursued to just north of this area; a little further east, the Isle of Dogs may have got its name from the royal hunting kennels which were kept there. Wapping became a riverside village specialising in ships (sail-making, boat-building, chandlers etc) and catering for sailors (lodging-houses, entertainments and taverns). In the High Street alone there were 36 taverns by 1750 and by the early nineteenth century, when seafaring had been vastly expanded, largely through the work of the press gangs (about 1780–1815), there was an astounding total of 140 taverns; many were just drinking dens. The area became overcrowded, leading to vice, violence and epidemics. Pepys frequently mentioned disturbances down at Wapping (he was Secretary to the Admiralty), and Dr Johnson observed with his usual succinctness that one could see ways of life that 'very few could even imagine'.

Continuing along the High Street, openings to the right give opportunities to look across the Thames to the great docks and warehouses of Bermondsey. Soon we come to the range of warehouses called Standard Wharf, complete with loading bays and cranes. Until the late 1870s the High Street was only one carriageway wide but then the road was enlarged by the Metropolitan Board of Works and that encouraged firms to construct huge, new warehouses – and handsome they are too.

Beside the grim aspect of Wapping there was a respectable side: the presence of skilled craftsmen, reliable tradesmen and distinguished sea captains. The superb terraces of Regency houses which face each other at Wapping Pier Head (right) are examples of the very fine homes which were built for those in command. These terraces were built in 1811 by the London Dock Company for their officials; they are now privately occupied as three- to four-bedroom houses. With their perfect proportions and captivating rounded ends, the terraces look even more impressive from the river. Indeed, that was the intention for where the lawns now run was the original entrance,

44

Pier Head, Wapping

Wapping Entrance, into London Docks; ships would sail in and out between the terraces. This entrance was filled in in 1958 after the lock gates had been damaged by barges. At the northernmost part of the lawns there is now a wall running across but beyond that there used to be the Wapping Basin (filled in 1968–70) which led, in turn, into the Western Dock (filled in 1980–82). The Basin now holds the playing fields of Wapping Sports Centre.

Next on the right is the Town of Ramsgate pub, so named to attract fishermen from Ramsgate when they came to London to sell their catches. This pub and the Prospect of Whitby (further along) are the only survivors of the old taverns. Both are now very fashionable public houses, but that was not always so – not in the days when the Town of Ramsgate was known as the Red Cow. It was here in 1688 that Judge Jeffreys, the 'hanging judge', was tracked down while trying to flee the country, following the example of his king, James II. Disguised as an ordinary seaman, he obtained a passage on a ship berthed in the Pool of London and bound for Hamburg. With time to spare before sailing he went ashore for a drink but he was recognised and he was nearly lynched by the mob before troops arrived from the Tower of London. He died there the following year aged forty-four. A gibbet has been set up on the pub's riverside terrace. From here can also be seen Wapping Old Stairs, one of the few remaining river landing-places which used to exist at every available spot.

Beside the pub is Oliver's Wharf. It has a Gothic feel about its design; it has been converted to flats and the old lettering of the wharf's name retained. A nice touch has been to keep the sign 'keep away from the cranes' – the cranes are still there. Opposite is a small walled garden which was the graveyard to the parish church of St John's. Now go up Scandrett Street. This church dates from 1790, replacing the earlier one of 1617. Together with the attractive buildings beside it, it was bombed during the war, the weed-grown bombed space now one of the few wartime scars left in London. The church tower, which has a very worthy lead-covered Baroque dome, and the adjoining buildings are listed for preservation. Behind St John's in Green Bank is an exceptionally fine Roman Catholic church designed as a Romanesque Basilica by Tasker in 1879. St Patrick's was unusual for its Classical style at a time when Gothic was at the climax of its popularity.

Scandrett Street continues into Tench Street where (left) there is the new Wapping Sports Centre (1980) built over and around the old Wapping Basin. It offers a wide range of sports and during holiday time children are invited to join their interesting scheme called Try-a-Sport. The centre still uses one of the old Harland and Wolff workshops: a fine curved building where heavy engineering was undertaken. The foundry wheel is on display. The centre is surrounded by parts of the original walls. Magnificent gate piers and iron gates testify to the grandness of conception and the security which was offered to traders when Britain was at her apogee as a maritime nation.

Return to the High Street and turn left. Now comes the terrific range of St John's Wharves, their gantries going across the road. On the right is the new Metropolitan Police Boatyard and then a small public garden. From here there is an invigorating view across the two sections of the Pool of London, known as the Lower Pool (left) and the Upper Pool. Across and to the left can be seen the spire of St Mary's (1714), the parish church of Rotherhithe. The impression which we get today, with lower buildings clustered around the church, is still that of a riverside village. Directly across is another famous old pub with associations with Judge Jeffreys, the Angel. Jeffreys would sit and take his dinner while watching executions taking place on this side at Execution Dock. Along the eastern wall of the garden is Wapping New Stairs.

Back on the High Street turn right and we come to another building of St John's Wharves, a quite astounding restoration, consisting of honey-coloured London stock brick and purple-brown bricks outlining doors and windows, their corners rounded off to minimise chipping. The road surface has its original cobbled surface and runs between towering warehouses. King Henry's Stairs used to lead to the old Tunnel Pier which was demolished about 1961. Nearby was the site of Execution Dock.

The sites which were allocated for public executions were all placed outside the City walls, except for the one on Tower Hill. Each site dealt with a particular type of offender and had different methods of execution. At Tyburn (Marble Arch) common criminals were hanged, heretics were burned at Smithfield, the cream of society were beheaded at Tower Hill and pirates were hanged in chains at Execution Dock where they were left until three tides had washed over them. The most distinguished recipient of this treatment was Captain Kidd in 1701. The number of offences which carried the death penalty soared from fifty during the seventeenth century to more than two hundred by 1819.

Further along is Gun Wharf. It has been completely restored and converted to residential use (1984) ranging from studio apartments to penthouse. One interesting feature is that planning permission required that a riverside walkway should be provided. This will become a public path once similar walkways have been provided all the way along the river.

Opposite Gun Wharf is Wapping Lane which divided the Eastern from the Western section of London Docks, the road crossing the channel which joined the sections together. All was filled in during 1980–82. Lovers of Victorian churches should visit St Peter's, Wapping Lane (Pownall 1866) which

Betjeman described as having 'great emotional appeal'. It is true. The sombre exterior, still coated with dockyard soot, hides an interior of surpassing beauty and richness of colour. It is usually open, but if it is not apply at one of the doors under the arch as you approach the church.

Continuing from Gun Wharf we pass Wapping underground station on the Metropolitan line which goes under the Thames to Rotherhithe. It uses what was one of the most famous engineering feats in the world. Known as the Thames Tunnel (1823–43), it was the first tunnel ever to be built underwater. The incredible achievement of burrowing through soft, oozing mud was made possible by the tunnelling shield invented (1818) by Marc Brunel (1769–1849). He was later assisted by his brilliant son Isambard Kingdom Brunel (1806–59) when only twenty-one. The principle of the shield was to divide up the area which was to be excavated into tiny sections, each being dug out, bricked up and completed before moving ahead. This principle survives even in the latest methods today. Nevertheless, the tunnel collapsed on numerous occasions which, together with financial delays, resulted in the work taking twenty years to complete.

So much was spoken and written and even sung about the project that it was nicknamed 'The Great Bore'. But such was the interest that when only halfway to completion a great dinner was held in the tunnel with 170 guests plus the band of the Coldstream Guards. It was opened by Queen Victoria. An elegant rotunda with spiral staircase stood on the site of the present station; the Queen descended, walked through the tunnel and knighted the older Brunel. After the first flush of fame the tunnel soon proved to be unsuccessful in its original conception as a traffic route; it failed to attract horse-drawn carts and had to settle for pedestrians. But it was still a tourist attraction and annual fairs were held in it; some forty thousand people attended a fair in 1853. In 1865, however, it was sold to the East London Railway Company and just over ten years later the first trains started to run through it. The postscript to this story is that, of the many deaths which occurred during construction of the tunnel, the majority of men died from diseases caused by the putrid water of the river.

The High Street now bears left but we take the first turning to the right, Wapping Wall, with some very fine warehouses; it is quite remarkable how much is still left. The road has a fine, cobbled surface and runs past the Metropolitan Wharf. This has all been renovated and painted a spectacular carmine-red, a traditional bright colour associated with river craft. The building contains a number of artists' studios which are let on short licences. There is also the Riverside Gallery specialising in 'art for offices'. The whole complex is known as Riverside Studios and is the Arts Centre of Wapping.

A short distance further along is the Prospect of Whitby, perhaps London's most famous pub. Originally it was known as the Devil's Tavern for it was the haunt of pirates and smugglers, but in 1777 it changed to its present name, taking the name of a ship which regularly tied up alongside. Pepys was a frequent visitor (the Pepys Society meets here), as was Dickens and the great marine artists Turner and Whistler. It has been a famous landmark for sailors since it opened in 1520 and is marked on marine charts of the area. Over the entrance is a list of twenty-one monarchs who have reigned during its existence beginning with Henry VIII. Beside it is the Pelican Stairs.

Wapping Wall crosses over the entry into Shadwell New Basin (1860s) which, with the Eastern and Western Docks already mentioned, completed the London Docks. An unusual counterbalanced bascule bridge takes the road over a channel, and down to the left is a pretty L-shaped terrace of nine new houses. Behind them is the spire of St Paul's, the parish church of old Shadwell Village. This basin, the only part of London Docks to remain as an enclosed water-space, is being developed under an environmental improvement scheme as a centre for water sports. In the summer an open-air youth club uses it for canoeing, sailing and other activities. Enter (right) King Edward VII Memorial Park which was opened by George V in 1922: a small park but nicely planted and with a terrace running parallel to the road. There is a refreshment pavilion and a paddling pool. It stands on the site of the Shadwell Fish Market, closed down during World War I.

The development of the market and the dockland only increased the miserable overcrowding and slum conditions of the area. People involved in the shipping trades were obliged to live near the water so the destruction of their houses and streets did not make them move away. Contemporary reaction, even though it was hardened to the harshness of life, was nevertheless not unmoved by the hellish conditions of Wapping and Shadwell. Epidemics were worse here than anywhere else in London and in the dreadful outbreak of cholera in 1866 three-quarters of the deaths occurred here. In 1842 an area survey showed that the average lifespan was forty-five years for the professional classes, thirty-seven for tradesmen and only twenty-two for labourers and servants. These figures are not surprising when it is considered that there was no drainage here until after 1850.

The path through the park leads to a circular structure, with the initials LCC boldly incorporated into the wrought-iron window screens. There is a similar structure on the other side of the river and these are ventilator shafts for the Rotherhithe Tunnel. Built (1904–8) by the London County Council at a cost of £2 million, it was constructed for the same purpose as Brunel's tunnel – road traffic. Over three thousand people had to leave their homes to make way for the tunnel but, unlike the case of the London Docks, they were rehoused.

Next to the ventilator stands a tablet, dated 1922, inscribed: 'In memory of Sir Hugh Willoughby, Stephen Borough, William Borough, Sir Martin Frobisher and other navigators who, in the latter half of the sixteenth century, set sail from this reach of the River Thames near Ratcliff Cross to explore the Northern Seas.' This reach is indeed a sight to rouse the adventurous spirit. We are at a bend of the river and it curves away from us into tremendous vistas of water as we take our length-way view. Directly across there used to be a maze of masts, funnels and cranes at the Surrey Commercial Docks, Rotherhithe, long since filled in.

Continue to the Free Trade Wharf, ahead, which contains a fine cluster of eighteenth-century buildings. The main entrance, up on the Highway, has a low colonnaded front flanked by large, shallow arches in the Soane style. Stone stairs are to the left. The whole ensemble is thoroughly memorable and it bears the arms, which are original, of the oldest of London's

50

dock companies, the East India Company.

Retrace your steps, now going west along the Highway, and make for the spire of St Paul's, the parish church of Shadwell. It has long been associated with seamen since it began as a chapel of ease in 1656 on land leased from St Paul's Cathedral and became the parish church in 1669. The church registers are crowded with the names of sea captains and their wives. Captain Cook was an active parishioner, and his son James was baptised here; as was the mother of Thomas Jefferson, and Walter Pater the novelist. John Wesley preached here on a number of occasions but not in this particular building. The church was rebuilt in 1820 (John Walters) and was described by Pevsner as 'cheaply built and designed without fire'. In fact at £27,000 it was the second most expensive church of its time (after St Pancras New Church) and was one of the Waterloo Churches which, to a high degree, were of distinguished design. Pevsner, however, did not see it in its present livery. The London Dock Development Corporation (LDDC) and the London Borough of Tower Hamlets have collaborated in the restoration of the church and the Institute which faces it and have produced an exquisite enclave within the churchyard and its surrounding wall. But not without some attendant tragedy. While scaffolding was covering the outside walls thieves had easy access to the roof which they stripped of its lead. Parishioners courageously then assembled community help to repair interior rain-damage. A key can be obtained from the eighteenth-century rectory next to the Institute.

Cross over the main road and then continue to reach the great Hawksmoor church of St George-in-the-East (1715–23). In the 1850s there were dreadful scenes during Sunday services when the congregation, angered by the incumbent's form of service, created disturbances. Shouting 'No Popery', they threw rubbish at the altar, aimed pea-shooters at the rector and sang 'Rule Britannia'. Looking at the church now, superb in its recent restoration – an unworldly white – it is hard to believe that on one occasion two hundred police stood inside to keep the peace. Together with St Anne's Limehouse and Christ Church Spitalfields, St George's completes Hawksmoor's titanic triumvirate known as his Stepney Churches. Each church requires a chapter, and a visit, on its own.

Continuing west, take the second turning right (Wellclose Street) and enter Wellclose Square. Originally laid out as a square in the sixteenth century, it was a distinguished address for sea captains. It was especially popular with the Danish who had their own church where St Paul's School now stands. It was calamitous that the remaining houses in this celebrated square should have been cleared away but the school is a Victorian Gothic gem. It was built for seamen's children in 1869. Heading off to the north-west corner is Grace's Alley where a theatre has stood, with various rebuildings, since 1826. The last building of 1859, which was known as Wilton's Music Hall, is to be restored. The whole of this area was within the liberties of the Tower of London, which meant that for a fee prisoners at the Tower were at liberty to take a brief spell of freedom within the area.

Carry on into Cable St, where ropes and cables were made, and turn left (due west) for Tower Hill station.

RIVER LEA

Introduction

In prehistoric times vast forests covered the land north of the Thames and the area contained an immense network of rivers and streams with the River Lea as the principal source of one of the most complex networks of all. The River Lea begins at Leagrave near Luton and near the most celebrated of primordial tracks, the Icknield Way. It runs east towards Hertford and Ware and then follows an almost due south course till it meets the Thames on the east side of the Isle of Dogs. Throughout it gives rise to many tributaries which double-back in places into a lacework of watery paths, for example Waltham Cross and Bow.

Twenty-five thousand years ago primitive people made extensive use of these waterways as they were the only practical means of moving about. The principal rivers were mostly larger than they are today and made an infinite number of small routes navigable for shallow boats; the Hackney Brook, which no longer exists, could flood to a width of 70ft (21m). This web of streams would overflow at times and create large areas of marsh, swamp and reeds with their attendant colonies of wildfowl. Life was abundant, and judging by the large numbers of flint tools discovered and the evidence of many encampments which have been traced, a sizeable population of hunters lived off the forests, marshes and rivers.

About 3,000BC primitive farming began and the forests were cleared from the lighter soil areas to the north as well as from the river banks to the south. A rudimentary pattern was established which would be followed in future development: extensive agricultural land to the north and commercial ribbon development along the river towards the Thames.

Such was the pattern of development around the Lea throughout the Roman period. Their armies crossed and re-crossed the Lea to and from Colchester, Stratford (ie street-ford) being the place where the *street* from Aldgate crossed over the *ford* on the River Lea. Boudicca blazed her way across it to attack Roman *Londinium,* and the ancient British tribes of the Trinovantes and the Catuvellauni skirmished with one another across the Lea which was their boundary.

No major changes occurred until the ravages of the Danish raids in the ninth century which met the stiff resistance of Alfred the Great. In 886 Alfred and Guthrum drew up a treaty defining the line which separated the areas of Saxon law from Danish law, known as the Danelaw, and part of that line ran up the River Lea. The Lea now became Alfred's forward line not of defence but of attack. In 894, after the Battle of Benfleet (near Southend), the defeated Danes sailed up the Lea to Ware which was in striking distance of Alfred's army in London. But Alfred's brilliant counterattack was based entirely upon his use of the river. He dammed it. Altering its course, he left the Danish ships high and dry thus destroyed their mobility, on which the Dane's particular style of warfare depended. Under his son Edward, Hertford was turned into a powerful fortified town that achieved great strategic importance against the Danelaw in the tenth century. Situated at the confluence of four rivers, the Mimram, Rib, Beane and the Lea, Hertford's castle, although now ruined, reminds us of a great stand against a would-be invader, the Danes, which succeeded.

The Domesday Book is our next important landmark because it indicates the considerable extent of the fisheries on the Lea; also its watermills, maltings, vineyards and beehives. By the thirteenth century there was extensive industry along the Lea; barges were busy for they were the only practical means of transporting huge quantities of corn, wheat, barley and hay, the roads being few and almost impassable for wheeled traffic. The maltings at Ware, recorded in Domesday, are probably the longest continuing industrial tradition in England, which indicates the excellent river communications with the wheat fields to the north.

In 1613 Sir Hugh Myddleton, a Welshman and a goldsmith, completed his extraordinarily beneficent scheme for bringing fresh water from Amwell near Ware, and later from the Lea, to London 38 miles (60km) away. The Lea thus became the focal point of life-giving water supplies which led to the great reservoirs of north-east London and the Lea Valley Water Company which functions to this day. Forty years later in 1653 Isaak Walton published his discourse on 'the contemplative man's recreation'. *The Compleat Angler* is an idyllic account of a five-day fishing trip along the River Lea from Tottenham to Ware and back. Walton writes with particular eloquence on the quiet unspoilt charm of the river which no doubt accounts for what Charles Lamb described as the book's 'spirit of innocence, purity and simplicity of heart', qualities which we can associate with the river today in places nor far from the North Circular Road itself.

The eighteenth century saw considerable development of the Lea and its neighbouring rivers. Dredging and widening improved many sections, while difficult or excessively winding sections were bypassed by 1765 with artificial cuts, or navigations, to provide more direct routes. New industries developed: silk-spinning, the superb china produced at Bow, wood mills, basket-making and straw-platting. The Lea's network of small streams, enclosing large damp areas, gave an ample growth of willow and rushes for basket-making, while straw hats, even straw coats, became almost an obsession with the population at large. Nimble-fingered girls could earn the incredible sum of five shillings a day in 1800.

During the nineteenth century malting and brewing became the principal industries. Ware was the centre with thirty-three maltings as early as 1788, and the Lea and its tributary the Stort were the main routes for transportation. It is not surprising therefore that there was also a prodigious number of pubs in Ware with an estimate of one pub to every fifty men. The timber trade also developed rapidly and this has remained the principal commercial use of the Lea today; enormous logs are transported to the saw mills at Hertford and other riverside timberyards, although road transportation is increasing.

For centuries London's 'Eastenders' have escaped to the Lea for recreation and it has a favoured place in Cockney affections. Since the last war, however, the drastic decline in commercial work on the river has posed the question whether the river's extensive network should be retained at all; the Fleet River, after all, was ultimately submerged in underground pipes. However, it was the Lea's ancient tradition as London's most spacious and amenable resort that led to the establishment of the Lee Valley Regional Park Authority in 1967. The Lee Valley Park extends for an astonishing 23 miles (36km) from Ware to the Thames, with a total of nine recreational centres offering an impressive range of activities, including Pickett's Lock and Eastway sports centres. The Lea has now taken on a new life as London's principal recreation resort.

Finally, the River Lea makes an important contribution to London's water supply delivering 14 per cent of the water consumed by Londoners. Under the Thames Water Authority, the Lea is associated with the stupendous series of reservoirs at Walthamstow; only 5 per cent of its daily flow is left for navigation, the rest being extracted for the water supply. In addition to the Lee Valley Park, the Thames Water Authority also makes a major contribution to recreation with its own facilities for fishing, birdwatching, sailing and, of course, walking.

In its 58 mile (93km) course, from Leagrave to the Thames, the River Lea is seen to be a London waterway second only to the Thames. Historically, commercially and recreationally the advantage has, in the past, mostly been for those living in the eastern suburbs, but the enormous future potential of the Lee Valley Park will surely spread this advantage to an ever-increasing extent throughout the metropolis.

5 Bow Back Rivers
4 miles (6.4km) (circular walk)

Trains: Bromley-by-Bow underground station
Buses: 86, 108, S2
Map: OS sheet no 177

This is a circular route that will take you through a remarkable maze of waterways with surprising contrasts between heavily used commercial roads and the quietest of rural backwaters. The waterways are partly man-made, partly natural, with areas given to flooding but turned to good commercial account by a number of 'cuts'. In broad terms we are dealing with the old River Lea and its more practical version in the Lea Navigation. There is still a great deal of industry in the area, cleaner and quieter than it used to be, and still some working barges especially for carrying copper to the rolling mills at Enfield and logs to timber mills at Hertford and to other mills along the Lea. But, of course, this is only a fraction of the traffic which used to serve industries with waterside premises. Stout iron bollards are to be seen everywhere, most of them now nestling within a camouflage of wild flowers. Even so, the river banks are well maintained on the whole. A stretch such as the Pudding Mill River still has its banks well shored up although they are now wildly overgrown.

We begin at the Bow Locks. From Bromley-by-Bow station cross straight over the main road and turn right. Pass The Rising Sun pub and take the next turning (no name) left. If you are going by car locate Gillender Street E3 on a map of London. It is a small service road running off the east side of the Blackwall Tunnel Northern Approach. Study the map carefully before setting out because the traffic is of motorway speed and intensity and should you overshoot this turning you will have a terrible problem to get back again – so be warned! Assuming all has gone well, motorists should continue along Gillender Street, pass The Rising Sun pub on your left and take the next turning (no name) which brings you down to the lock area.

On your left is the long straight stretch of the Limehouse

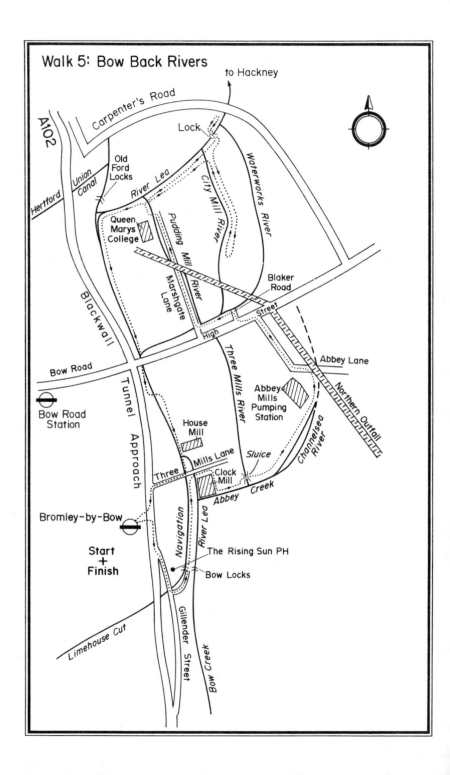

Walk 5: Bow Back Rivers

to Hackney

A102

Carpenter's Road

Lock

Hertford Union Canal

Old Ford Locks

River Lea

City Mill River

Waterworks River

Queen Marys College

Pudding Mill River

Blaker Road

Blackwall

Marshgate Lane

Street

High

Bow Road

Abbey Lane

Three Mills River

Northern Outfall

Bow Road Station

Tunnel Approach

House Mill

Abbey Mills Pumping Station

Channelsea River

Three Mills Lane

Sluice

Clock Mill

Bromley-by-Bow

Navigation

Abbey Creek

Start + Finish

River Lea

The Rising Sun PH

Bow Locks

Limehouse Cut

Gillender Street

Bow Creek

Cut and on the right is the lower reach of the River Lea which is known as Bow Creek. Walk along past the lock-keeper's house and administration offices and go up over the footbridge. At the top of the footbridge you get an excellent view which shows the great extent of waterways which we shall be exploring. Looking downstream the Bow Creek reaches the Thames in just over 2 miles (3.2km) in a series of immense loops, or bows, which double-back on themselves to an exceptional degree. Looking upstream you see the Lea to the right and, separated by a wall, the Navigation to the left. Further up, and swinging out of sight to the right, is the Abbey Creek.

Cross the bridge taking the path between the two parallel rivers. Go under the two-arch white road bridge and then under the railway bridge which carries the District and Metropolitan lines. Here you find the Lea curving grandly to the left and Abbey Creek running off to the right between high walls.

Directly in front are the superb buildings which are known as Three Mills. Continue ahead to the small bridge and turn right. The whole of this area was used by watermills, the ones here being operated by the rise and fall of the tides. Domesday Book referred to nine mills in this area. In 1134 Stratford Abbey was founded on the banks of the nearby Channelsea River (on our route). The abbey owned the mills on this site when it was closed down by Henry VIII in 1538. This area was where most of the flour was produced for London's bakers, who later objected when bread was also baked in Stratford and Bow at prices which undercut the City's tradesmen. By the end of the eighteenth century distilling had also become an important industry at the watermills so it is in keeping with tradition that Charringtons now occupy part of this site.

Today there are not three but only two mills: House Mill and Clock Mill. Clock Mill, the more spectacular of the two with its attractive octagonal clocktower and two black cones, dates from 1817, late Georgian, although the clocktower, clock and bell date from 1750. It has been excellently restored for which it received a conservation award in 1974 and is now discreetly occupied by Charringtons' offices. It is listed Grade II. House Mill, displaying a plaque dated 1776, is listed Grade I and is regarded as one of the finest remaining buildings of the

Clock Mill

early industrial revolution. Both mills stand above water channels through which ebb tides drove the millwheels. The buildings are redolent of the age of craftsmen, of long apprenticeships and devoted attention to nature, the massive wooden beams, brick and cast-iron evoking the traditions of centuries. House Mill has been considered for a number of years for restoration to a working mill. In the meantime its windows have been boarded up with fake panes of glass painted on, so well done that it is difficult to believe that they are not genuine. One aspect of conservation which is not generally known is that other relics in addition to buildings can be listed. Here the old-world cobbled lane between the mills is also listed Grade II—looking at it for a moment one can imagine the clatter of horses' hoofs.

Pass Clock Mill on your right then turn first right down the narrow alley; the large modern building on your left, which fits well into the surroundings, is a bonded warehouse. The path now takes us around the other side of Clock Mill, showing an attractive iron crane and an overhanging wooden attic which contained a hoist. We now follow round the north edge of Abbey Creek and cross over the sluice at Prescott Channel, the waters rushing beneath us. Turn right towards the Abbey Creek and continue again along its north side; the pathway is defined more by use than design. We are now in Mill Meads, formerly the meadows belonging to the old Abbey's mill. It is a delightful spot filled with wild flowers in spring and summer. The far bank shows present-day industry in its clean and quiet aspect; there is the same sense of orderly activity that we felt back at the old mills. The path becomes very narrow in summer as luxuriant growth pushes across the way, but all along we can still see the built-up edge of the creek from former, more affluent times. At low tide the exposed river mud gives off a pungent odour which only serves to make us feel even further from civilisation although we are in the centre of a huge rectangle bounded by some of East London's busiest commercial roads.

Up above you will see powerlines, and when you draw level with the first pylon which comes up on your left make a short detour towards it. Here you will see a building that is both grand and bizarre; the brightly coloured 'Renaissance' dome of Abbey Mills Pumping Station is set like a palace within watermeadows. It was designed by Sir Joseph Bazalgette in 1868 and was an integral part of his vast system of underground drains. This building pumps sewage from as far away as the Victoria Embankment. Inside the pumping station high galleries, intended for access to oiling points on the huge beam engines, were visited in Victorian times by devoted admirers of human enterprise who would sit enthralled, gazing upon the gleaming engines below. Stratford Abbey stood upon this site and the Channelsea River, which drove the Abbey's mill, begins just where we return to our path and carry on. You soon go between concrete walls and reach a flight of steps which takes you to the top of the Northern Outfall where you turn left.

Move over to the right and find the entrance to a flight of stairs which takes you down to Abbey Lane. Turn right under the outfall and cross to the left side of the road. This brings you to the entrance gates of the pumping station where again you can see the attractive buildings and grounds. Abbey Lane curves right and left before we see water again. Reaching High Street, Stratford E15, go left on to the bridge and look south along the pleasant stretch of Three Mills River; it runs down to House Mill and Clock Mill. Crossing over to the other side of the main road, you will see Blaker Road where we join up with a wonderful complex of waterways. To the right runs Waterworks River (no path), ahead is City Mill River (which we will visit from its other end) and to the left the City Mill Lock, now very dilapidated. Go down the steps to the lock and continue along the path beside the river.

At the next bridge turn right along Marshgate Lane where (right) you come to the Pudding Mill River, a canal which is now disused. Its water is covered with a thick crust of green weed and a winter's supply of firewood. The canal has now been cut off at the railway bridge but continue under the ubiquitous Northern Outfall and you pick it up again on the left side. There is an attractive curved wooden bridge from which you can see that, in spite of heavy overgrowth, the banks are still in good condition. This area was the Stratford Marsh and now contains good modern industrial units and, to the left, Queen Mary's College. The road curves to the left down to a towpath and continues ahead to a junction with the River Lea where you turn right along its south bank.

This is the original course of the river and it winds round in a huge sweep to join the Navigation just beyond Hackney Marsh Recreation Ground. It is known locally as The Loop and is a favourite fishing spot. The towpath has regularly placed iron bollards, almost hidden when in summer's growth, which are silent proof of the river's once busy industry. In the ninth century the Danish invaders sailed up this river on their way to attack Ware and Hertford. Around a bend we suddenly come upon the junction with the City Mill River, a fine open space like a waterway roundabout. Cross the steeply arched iron bridge and continue ahead, the river to your left. We come to the disused Carpenter's Road Lock; its fine radial gates, which swung upwards to allow traffic to go underneath, should not have been allowed to deteriorate. Cross over the next bridge, going right up to the wall, and follow the delightful path, the trees meeting overhead, with good views down Waterworks River. At Carpenter's Road we have to retrace our steps as there is no access to the river going north at this point. When you return to the steeply arched iron bridge do not at first cross over but turn left down City Mill River, the water on your right. Here we have perhaps the finest embankments of our walk – and if you go in blackberrying time, just about the finest fruit you will see.

On your return, this time cross the iron bridge, keeping the River Lea to your right. This brings you back to Pudding Mill River where, again, you cross a small bridge and continue to the junction with the Navigation and the rushing waters of Old Ford Locks. The locks are over to your right and are worth exploring (take the bridge across) before turning south along the Navigation. We now walk parallel to the motorway which we join at the High Street. Cross straight over the High Street and continue ahead for 50yd (45m) before turning left to the towpath which is now on the right side of the river.

At the next bridge we are back at the old mills. If you wish to return to Bow Locks carry straight on, but if you want the buses or station turn right passing the new Tesco store. This is a particularly pleasing building opened in 1983, long and low with beautifully mottled bricks and two corner turrets which are a nice reference to the twin cones on Clock Mill. Turn left along the front of the store where there is a bus stop; Bromley-by-Bow station is across on the right.

6 Bow Road or Hackney Wick to Tottenham Hale

5 miles (8km) from Bow Road
4 miles (6.4km) from Hackney Wick

Trains: Bow Road underground station
        Hackney Wick (British Rail)
Buses: For Bow Road: 10, 25, 86, 108
      For Hackney Wick: 236, S3 (but check times)
Map: OS sheet no 177

If you are starting from Bow Road turn right on leaving Bow Road station and go to the roundabout. Access to the towpath is at the north-east junction. Comments on the section between Bow and Old Ford Locks may be found at the end of the previous walk. It is well worth the little extra distance to start from Bow for we thereby take in part of the Back Rivers, the fine lock area and a broad and serene part of the Lea Navigation leading up to Hackney Wick. You then pick up the walk again after the next paragraph.

If, however, you are starting from Hackney Wick turn left on reaching the road and follow the pavement all the way to Carpenter's Road Bridge. Go over the bridge and cross to the south side which takes you down to the towpath. Continue south along the towpath for about 100yd (90m) to the Hertford Union Canal which you will see over to the right; this is a fine triangular water junction.

The Hertford Union Canal is an absolutely straight piece of water and was intended as a short-cut between the Regent's Canal and the Lea. It was made in 1830 by Sir George Duckett and is often referred to as Duckett's Canal. Unlike the Limehouse Cut which was made in 1770 as a direct link between the Thames and the Lea, the Hertford Union Canal was a commercial offshoot of the Regent's Canal. It shortened the journey from the Regent's Canal to the Lea by some 4 miles (6.4km) and avoided the congestion of Limehouse Basin. From a position looking directly along the Hertford Union Canal you will see the first of its three locks and a suggestion of its quiet charm when it runs, later on, beside Victoria Park.

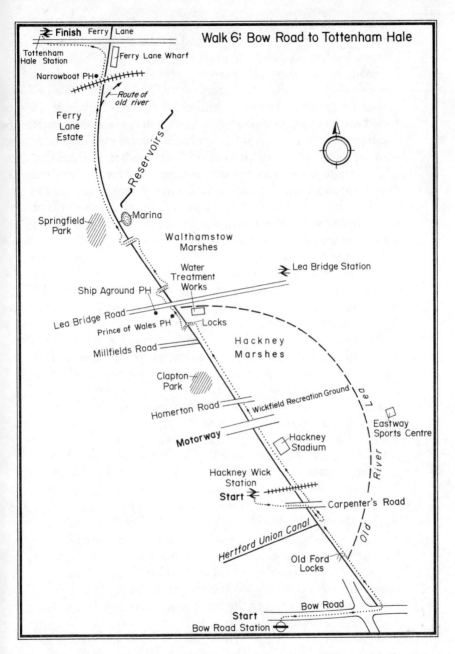

Walk 6: Bow Road to Tottenham Hale

Now retrace the short distance back to Carpenter's Road Bridge (river to the left) and go under it, as well as under the railway bridge which serves Hackney Wick station. The river is broad, straight and well shored-up by a system of interlinking metal piles backed with concrete. The towpath here becomes quite a narrow track, and the frequent changes from broad made-up surface to bumpy path will remain with us. A number of new and handsome factories can be seen (corrugation seems to be the favoured motif) but it will be noticed that not only are there scarcely any loading bays for waterborne goods but that hardly any windows exist either. Modern buildings now have their backs to the river and to reduce the areas of possible entry and vandalism they present merely ventilation intakes to the once-glorious riverway.

Hackney Stadium (opened 1932) can be seen over to the right, the first indication of the extensive sporting facilities which are to come. Further to the east behind the stadium (and out of sight to us) is the Eastway Centre of the Lea Valley Park, which has a multitude of sporting activities available.

After passing beneath the old Eastway and the twin motorway bridges, we pass (left) an enormous factory complex. It continues through various interesting new architectural styles for such a distance as to strike a comical connection with the product: the diminutive Lesney Matchbox Toys. To the right is Wick Field Recreation Ground.

Our route takes us along the Lea Navigation which is a canal following a more direct route than the original river which is winding circuitously around the far side of Hackney Marshes. The Navigation took its independent route back at Old Ford Locks and will join the river at the next locks at Lea Bridge. Artificial control of the river began over six hundred years ago. The enormous growth in the river's commercial traffic during the fifteenth century necessitated the good overall depth of water and the practical route made possible by man's intervention. The section which we are now entering is known as the Hackney Cut. In spite of the busy roads crossing over us, the factories and the distant tower blocks, the character of the river is rural. The towpath is richly edged with wild flowers and there is plenty of fishing. There is also abundant birdlife and at

The Hertford Union Canal (right) and the Lea Navigation

the appropriate time of year families of swans and their cygnets are often to be seen.

After the next bridge (Homerton Road), we enter the vast open tract (right) of Hackney Marshes. The shooting of wildfowl here continued into the nineteenth century, but since then football has been the main sport with many outstanding players being first spotted by talent-scouts while playing on these fields. During the nineteenth century rubbish was dumped here in an effort to reclaim the land, and during the last war, enormous quantities of rubble from bombed buildings were deposited here to complete the reclamation.

The next bridge, which is the end of Millfields Road, leads to a camping ground (right). Through the bridge and on the left was the site of the old Hackney Power Station which was demolished in 1983. So far our route has followed a nearly straight line so the distinctive left turn which lies ahead appears as a marked change. We are now bending around to the Pond Lane locks and a grand complex of channels as we join up with the old river. Here also are some superb reed-beds with magnificent bullrushes, reminding us of the primeval swamps that used to exist here.

Pond Lane flood gates are impressive. They are of the guillotine type and mostly are kept open: broad iron blades suspended above the water. Cross over the flood gates and continue on the left side to the weir. This is where the Navigation and river meet again after their long separation through the Hackney Marshes. Across the river can be seen the old Lea Bridge Water Treatment Works. Of special note is the main central building, its walls arcaded with five 'Norman' arches and a strong cornice under a broad, flat roof. The works were closed down in the early 1970s when the new Coppermills Works (about a mile away to the north) was inaugurated in 1972. The old Lea Bridge filter beds are now being used for various research projects. One is for breeding fish to supply the reservoirs with stock for the many sporting fishermen. There are two pubs here. The Prince of Wales stands beside the river and the Ship Aground is just behind the first pub; both serve food. Lea Bridge railway station is to the right along the main road (buses: 35, 48 and 55).

The towpath goes under the main road and continues along the left side of the river. Here are the marvellous lawns and avenues of trees of North Millfields Recreation Ground. The river turns sharp right and there is a sign pointing to the Kings Head beer garden down a narrow lane. The broad, clear towpath winds round and over a bridge to continue on the right side of the river and along Walthamstow Marshes. Now we are following the old river and shall continue to do so almost until the next main road. Walthamstow Marshes retain the character of wasteland and seem very wild compared to the fine landscaping that we have become used to. On the left is Springfield Park, where large numbers of Canada geese can sometimes be seen. The park rises steeply up from the river as it sweeps over Stamford Hill. It is attractively composed into spacious lawns marked off by avenues of trees, the considerable height being very much in contrast to the previous low-lying land. The waterside is especially lovely with its rich growth of trees, willows dipping into the water. Cross the next bridge and take the left bank. This passes the Springfield Marina which is part of the Lee Valley Park; it is a very large mooring which occupies an island site formed by a hook in the river. The Lea Rowing Club and Young Mariners' Canoeing Centre make this a much used highway for water sports. A small café serves light snacks, teas and ice creams.

Once past the marina, walk along the line of the Walthamstow Reservoirs that continue almost to Waltham Cross. Behind the high grassy bank on the right lies the West Warwick Reservoir which, with its East companion, dates from 1894; they are the oldest reservoirs in this group. The Ferry Lane housing estate (left) was built by the GLC (1980) but was transferred later to Haringey Borough Council. It is of deep red brick and has a slated upper storey. Much to its credit is its modest overall height and homely character, while the river façade, with its balconies and little yards with gates to the towpath, takes every advantage of the excellent position. There is a community centre and hall, shopping precinct and school. With six hundred units there is accommodation for two and a half thousand people – altogether an admirable addition to the riverside interest.

Just before the railway bridge, the old river sweeps off to the right but once again we follow the Navigation. Past the bridge there is the Narrowboat pub in similar style to the estate. Then come the nine enormous loading bays of Ferry Lane Wharf. Up on the main road, Ferry Lane, and to the left, is the GLC Supplies Department. Go along the front of this building for Tottenham Hale station (underground and British Rail) and buses 41 and 123.

7 Tottenham Hale to Waltham Cross
8 miles (12.8km)

Trains: Tottenham Hale (underground and British Rail)
Buses: 41, 123
Maps: OS sheet nos 177, 166

Our route follows to the very end of the Walthamstow Reservoirs. Turn left out of Tottenham Hale station and pass the GLC depot. On reaching the bridge take the stairs down to the towpath and to Tottenham Locks: a fine expanse of water and very popular with fisherman. Hale's Wharf (right) is now occupied by a number of firms including concrete, timber, electrical, paper and plaster trades. Sometimes the largest barges of 150 tons will be seen moored beside the wharf. To the left is Pymmes Brook which rises in Hadley Woods and flows through Southgate and Edmonton. It will accompany us for some distance well protected behind a metal fence. We are entering a section which contains a truly remarkable complex of waterways for transport, sewage, water supply and flood relief, matters which have concerned the Lea Valley for many centuries. The steep bank on the right contains the Lockwood Reservoir built in 1897 with the tops of waterworks buildings rising above the rim. When this reservoir was being constructed a Danish ship was discovered sunk in the mud of the old River Lea.

Tottenham achieved economic importance during the Middle Ages. Barges were plying all the way up from the Thames by the fourteenth century, and Ermine Street, the old Roman Road to York, ran through the village. But as the Lea was dredged and canalised and commerce could move further north towards the Hertfordshire wheat fields so Tottenham gradually lost this trade. Instead, it became a pleasant country retreat for affluent Londoners, retaining this character into the nineteenth century. Because of the clean air and opportunities for rural activities, it was especially recommended for private schools.

At the next lock, Stonebridge lock, cross over the bridge and the path continues along the right bank. This path takes us bet-

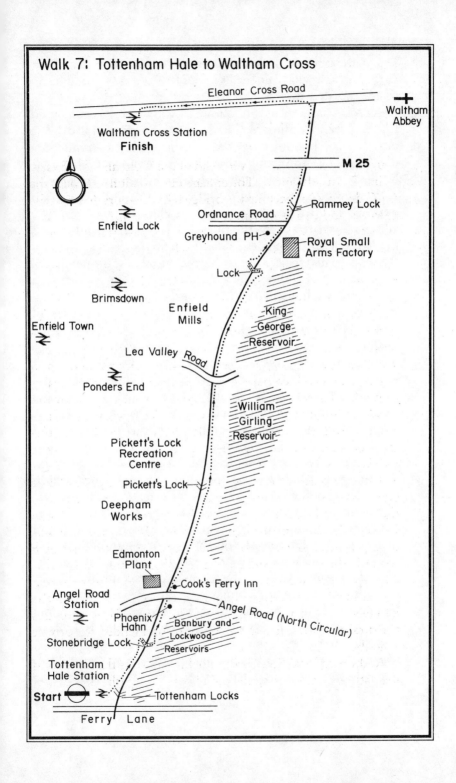

Walk 7: Tottenham Hale to Waltham Cross

Eleanor Cross Road

Waltham Abbey

Waltham Cross Station
Finish

M 25

Rammey Lock

Ordnance Road

Enfield Lock

Greyhound PH

Royal Small
Arms Factory

Lock

Brimsdown

Enfield
Mills

King
George
Reservoir

Enfield Town

Lea Valley Road

Ponders End

William
Girling
Reservoir

Pickett's Lock
Recreation
Centre

Pickett's Lock

Deepham
Works

Edmonton
Plant

Cook's Ferry Inn

Angel Road
Station

Angel Road (North Circular)

Phoenix
Hahn

Banbury and
Lockwood
Reservoirs

Stonebridge Lock

Tottenham
Hale Station

Start

Tottenham Locks

Ferry Lane

ween two waterways: the Navigation on the left and the River Lea on the right, with the tall reservoir bank beyond that. Over to the left you will again see Pymmes Brook now running away to the north-west as it gains its independence. Lockwood Reservoir comes to an end followed by low-lying ground used for the grazing of horses. The Banbury Reservoir (also 1897) now begins. Do not cross the next bridge but continue in a direct line with this path, although there is a fine view from the bridge of the immense water channels which converge here.

We now come to one of the largest and busiest factories on our route: the timberyards of Phoenix Hahn. Until about 1980 all the transport was via the river, but protracted trouble with the lightermen (bargemen) caused the firm to end a tradition that had existed for centuries. Further along, the Stonehill factory continues Edmonton's furniture-making industry, a tradition which includes many small firms and individual craftsmen. Opposite Stonehill's and on the left are acres of deserted covered yards no longer using their extensive riverside loading bays. Approaching the North Circular Road we see the impressive 'Egyptian' pylons of Lea Valley Viaduct as it crosses the river. Queensway, the furniture supermarket, has built a good-looking showroom with direct access to the main road, its cheerful use of colour bringing a metropolitan stylishness to the no-nonsense look of the older buildings. To the left along Angel Road is Angel Road railway station with buses 34, 102 and 144. We have completed about one-third of the walk. The station is named after a famous inn which no longer exists, but if we continue ahead Cook's Ferry Inn is very much alive. The towpath continues under the roadway. More timberyards indicate the amount of work which barge traffic has lost, and then comes the Edmonton Solid Waste Incineration Plant.

The Edmonton plant is a superb building by any standards, with the gigantic bulk of the incinerator and turbine blocks beneath a 300ft (90m) chimney; a raised exit road spirals around and out to the main road. Heat from the incinerators produces steam to drive turbines from which there is a sale of electricity to offset running costs. The site is beautifully landscaped and the structure is broken up into rectangles of different colours so as to reduce the effect of its overall size. On the

The refuse disposal plant at Edmonton

outside the cladding materials have self-cleaning plastic, tile and acrylic finishes to keep it always looking smart, colourful and hygenic. Never a puff of smoke comes from the chimney as all harmful grit is extracted by electrostatic process. It was completed in 1970 at a cost of £10 million.

Next, on the left, comes Deepham Sewage Treatment Works. Fourth largest in the GLC area, it handles forty million gallons daily and serves the area Tottenham–Enfield–Barnet–Chingford. A bacteriological purification process is used after which the inert sludge is either air-dried at a plant near Enfield lock and then used for fertilizer or pumped down to Beckton (the largest plant) and shipped out to sea for dumping. Crystal clear water is then returned via Pymmes Brook to the Lea at Tottenham Locks.

The towpath is now really delightful and helps to recall Edmonton's rural past when John Gilpin made his famous ride, immortalised in Cowper's poem. Cowper tells how Gilpin, 'a citizen of credit and renown', decided to take his wife and children 'unto the Bell at Edmonton' to celebrate their twentieth wedding anniversary, Gilpin following the chaise and pair on a borrowed horse. The beast, however, would not stop but bounded across the Lea and did a round trip to Ware and back adding 26 hair-raising miles (42km) to the journey. The poem achieved sensational popularity, and the actor John Henderson could attract huge audiences to London theatres to hear him recite it. In 1833, some hundred years later, Charles Lamb, the essayist, found the same rural character and tranquillity when he retired to the area; he died here in 1834.

The Navigation follows a straight line between the William Girling Reservoir on the right and the golf-course of Pickett's Lock Centre, another of the Lee Valley Park's recreation centres. The reservoir was begun in 1935 but, delayed by the war, it was not completed until 1951 when it was named after the chairman of the Metropolitan Water Board. A local farmer grazes his sure-footed sheep on the precipitous banks.

Behind the trees on the left bank, Lea Park Way can be seen running parallel to the river. This is a new road built as part of the Lee Valley Park and leads to Pickett's Lock Centre. Opened by the Duke of Edinburgh in 1973, the centre offers a new approach to a healthy way of life with nearly every sport catered for in pleasant surroundings, including badminton, basketball, football, bowls, hockey, netball, tennis, squash, swimming and roller skating. Particularly noteworthy is the indoor swimming pool, which has an irregular outline like a natural lake, and a beach with waves breaking realistically upon it. Camping grounds bring foreign visitors and an out-of-the-ordinary atmosphere for a sportsdrome.

Approaching the next bridge (Lea Valley Road), the William Girling Reservoir comes to an end. To the left is Ponders End railway station and buses 121, 149, 191 and 279. Across on the left bank can be seen a most attractive hook which returns to the main river beyond the bridge. Such a hook makes an easily controlled stream away from river traffic, so not surprisingly it has been the site of successive watermills over the centuries.

Ponders End has associations with the pioneer electrical industry. In 1886 Edison Swan started to make electric light bulbs in a factory in Duck Lees Lane, close by the river. Here also Sir Alexander Fleming invented the world's first radio valve, production starting in 1916. Twenty years later the first television tubes were produced. A spin-off from these thermionic valves was the famous Thermos vacuum flask.

The modern bridge (Lea Valley Road) leads to Enfield Town railway station (left) which was the site of a house of some historical interest. Built in 1672 it was the birthplace of Isaac D'Israeli, father of Benjamin Disraeli. It was demolished about 1906, but part of its façade can now be seen in the Victoria and Albert Museum. Later it was a school attended by John Keats. Another famous Enfield resident from 1842 to 1857 was the novelist Walter Pater.

Once past Lea Valley Road the King George V Reservoir (1913) begins. Coarse fishing, sailing and sub-aqua sports are enjoyed on this reservoir. The industrial works here along the left bank are interesting because of their mainly old-fashioned design and outmoded textures: darkened brick, weatherboarding and acres of rust. By contrast is a slim stainless-steel chimney belonging to the Enfield Rolling Mills, a plant which still receives sheets of copper by barge; the metal is sometimes piled up by the wharf. In spite of this industrial presence, families of ducks paddle in and out between the barges. Altogether this amounts to the most interesting industrial section of the walk: a leftover from past days before self-cleaning cladding set in. The river itself needs to be dredged for thick clusters of reeds and water. Picturesque no doubt but a hindrance to river traffic.

At the end of King George Reservoir there is the Small River Lea running off from a little junction to the left. It is a pretty stream that runs parallel to the main river before it joins again above Waltham Cross. The towpath leads on to Swan and Pike Road with the lock and lock-keeper's house (Lea Conservancy 1889) directly ahead. Bear left and the towpath continues along the left bank beside a fine, straight canal; a stop for the 121 bus is nearby.

Over to the right is an excellent Regency terrace of artisans' cottages called Government Row. Built in 1816, they were for workers at the famous Royal Small Arms Factory which was completed in 1804 in response to the need created by the Napoleonic Wars. The Lea Enfield rifle was made here, both river and town being recorded in its name. The RSAF began production with hand-made muskets; each one was unique and could not be repaired with standard parts. The Crimean War (1854–56) showed these weapons to be useless when so far from home. Mass-production methods were then adopted from America and this was the first British factory to do so. The chosen site, which is still behind Government Row, was a good one with access to waterpower and water transportation for explosives and raw materials and for the finished weapons to be shipped to the Tower of London. During the last war the Bren and Sten guns were also made here. There is an excellent museum open to the public which displays a historical collection of weapons including, of course, those originating from the RSAF.

Ahead is the Greyhound pub on the corner of Ordnance Road where, 600yd (54m) along, is Enfield Dock railway station. We now enter the open spaces of Rammey Marsh. Along the towpath several sites have been cleared and made into picnic spaces: gravel laid, trees planted and tables and benches set up. This is appropriate to this lovely, quiet reach –

rural and tree-lined and more richly grown with large chestnut and willow trees than on any previous section. The rushing of a weir brings us to a grand junction (right) with a flood relief channel and the old River Lea, succulent growth heralding the delights of Hertfordshire.

Keep on the left bank past Rammey Lock, with its modern lock-keeper's house, and the small boating centre of the Rammey Marsh Cruising Club. We go under the handsome, slender viaduct of the new M25 motorway and pass (left) the Lea Road Industrial Park with some attractive buildings. Many little watercourses abound. Hazelmere Marina occupies (left) a former commercial inlet and offers restaurant facilities. To the right are the parallel courses of the river and the Navigation. Leave the towpath at the main road (Eleanor Cross Road) where you can look back over the twin watercourses which we have followed for most of our route. From the other side of the road you can look over the Waltham Marshes where these courses diverge once again.

Should time permit, you could see (east, ten minutes' walk) the fine Waltham Abbey Church consecrated in 1060. It is supposedly where King Harold, last of the Saxon kings, was buried after the Battle of Hastings. It has fine Norman features as well as a superb Burne-Jones window. Otherwise, by going west for just over ½ mile (0.8km) you reach Waltham Cross railway station and buses 217, 217b, 242, 250 (Green Line 318, 329). On the way you cross the Small River Lea and pass a now rare corrugated-iron mission church.

RIVER WEY

Introduction

The Wey and the Lea have both had long and important histories as London's principal commercial rivers apart from the Thames. Their natural features were early improved upon with navigations, or canals, which cut across some of their more tortuous circumlocutions. Produce was thereby quickly brought to London, while country towns and villages which supplied the demand were in turn made prosperous. Both rivers, because of their excellence of design and construction and the enormous worth of the industries which they served, continued to work for their livings until comparatively recently. The Wey carried its last commercial shipment to Guildford in 1969.

Despite the demise of the watermill as essential industrial machinery by the early nineteenth century, the devastating effects of the railways in the mid-nineteenth century and of lorries, motorways and containers in the twentieth, the excellence (and beauty) of both rivers has kept them in use long after they were, in fact, commercially obsolete. In 1964 the Wey Navigation was handed over to the National Trust by its last commercial owner, Mr H.W. Stevens, and four years later the Commissioners for the Godalming Navigation did likewise. The whole 20 mile (32km) stretch is now part of our national heritage.

In appearance the two rivers are very different. The Lea smacks of the estuary: immense marshes stretch to the horizon, seagulls are frequent visitors and we are constantly entering busy industrial sites like a ship coming into port. The Wey, by contrast, is 'home': we have arrived and our walk takes us through our manorial grounds. From the very start of our walk at the Thames there is a consistency such as we associate with a private domain. As in any large estate, it has parts which may be distinguished one from another, but the overall sense is of passing within unseen walls, secluded and protected from the world.

This sense of seclusion, of being miles away from built-up areas, is quite astonishing as we walk along the Wey for we are, in reality, taking an ingenious route through some extensively populated areas. The origins of the Wey lie among a number of small streams that issue forth from Hampshire and south-west Surrey and they combine at Tilford to form the main river. It then flows eastward to Godalming from where, in 1760, it was made navigable. But a little over a hundred years earlier, in 1651, the journey from Guildford to the Thames had already been made navigable by Sir Richard Weston, a former owner of Sutton Place near Guildford. With a length of 15 miles (24km) from the Thames to Guildford and a further 5 miles (8km) to Godalming, the total length is similar to the journey on the Lea from the Thames to Hertford.

From Guildford the Wey flows through an opening in the North Downs, with views of distant heights following the route north. Much of the Navigation is earth banked and has become naturalised over the centuries. With the exception of some very straight sections, the Navigation is now indistinguishable from a natural river.

The two main sections of the Navigation are below Guildford and they shorten two big loops in the old river. The larger one is between Weybridge Town Lock and Newark Priory; the other one follows almost immediately after from Newark to Worsfold Flood Gates. Another section from Triggs Lock to the weir at Sutton Place is more to supply width and depth as the old river does not cover any greater distance than the Navigation at this point. Finally, a very short cut of about 500yd (450m) avoiding the loop at Jacobswell near Sutton Place is the last significant section of Navigation before Guildford. A noteworthy feature are the places where the Navigation is banked up high above the level of the land or, indeed, above the old river itself, the section south of Triggs Lock going past Send Church being the most spectacular example.

The locks have great individual character which makes them linger in the memory. Some of the most vivid memories are of those dream-like places – Walsham, Newark, Sutton Weir – where our thoughts are numbed by the hypnotic sound of rushing waters or the hazy atmosphere of watermeadows. The lock-keepers' cottages are also delightful. Although most of the locks are now unmanned, the cottages are nevertheless occupied, sometimes by people working for the National Trust, just to keep an eye on things. Particularly attractive are the cottages at Walsham Flood Gates and Triggs Lock. Everything is excellently maintained by the National Trust Workshops at Send. Lock gates can be seen by their dates in the 1970s and 1980s to have been renewed, while the magnificent floodgate machinery at Walsham (1931) and Sutton Place (1933) by Ransomes and Rapier of Ipswich is handsome in green livery. The River Wey is now smartly turned out for a comparatively new career in recreation and conservation under the watchful eye of the National Trust.

8 Weybridge to Send
8½ miles (13.5km)

Trains: Weybridge (British Rail)
Buses: 219; London Country 437, 461, 462; Green Line 725
   (alight at the Ship Hotel)
Maps: OS sheet nos 176, 186, 187

From Weybridge railway station turn right, go to the roundabout and turn left into Heath Road. The stop for buses 219 and 437 is immediately ahead. Alight at the Ship Hotel, a superb seventeenth-century building set back from the main road. Continue straight ahead past the hotel into Monument Green (there is a monument to your right); the continuation is called Thames Street. The Farnell Arms (left) is followed by the fine baroque columns of all that is left of the Portmore Estate (left). Immediately past The Old Crown (left) turn left along Church Walk which is between the pub and its small carpark.

 At the T-junction turn right and cross the small iron bridge which goes over the River Wey. Shortly afterwards bear left and carry on until you come to the water's edge. Here you turn

The River Wey at Weybridge

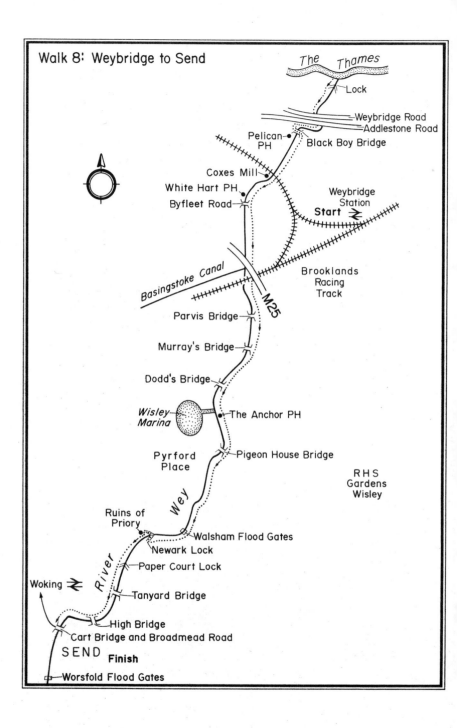

Walk 8: Weybridge to Send

The Thames
Lock
Weybridge Road
Addlestone Road
Pelican PH
Black Boy Bridge
Coxes Mill
White Hart PH
Byfleet Road
Weybridge Station
Start
Basingstoke Canal
M25
Brooklands Racing Track
Parvis Bridge
Murray's Bridge
Dodd's Bridge
Wisley Marina
The Anchor PH
Pyrford Place
Pigeon House Bridge
RHS Gardens Wisley
Wey
Ruins of Priory
Walsham Flood Gates
Newark Lock
Paper Court Lock
River
Woking
Tanyard Bridge
High Bridge
Cart Bridge and Broadmead Road
SEND Finish
Worsfold Flood Gates

right through a very small gate which brings you to Thames Lock. Cross the lock by the tiny bridge and then go left along the towpath, the water on your left. The lock utilises 100,000 gallons of water which pass through the lock in five minutes. The lock gates were renewed in 1981. We are now on the Wey Navigation. Soon we are accompanied by a little stream on the right (which leads to an overspill) and this pattern of streams and rivers coming and going will be with us throughout the walk. The whole area is very exciting both in sight and sound for the enormous presence of the Thames still has its influence upon the lower reaches of the Wey. A sharp bend in the river to the left brings us to the gardens of houses which are in Portmore Park Road; a delightful variety of modern bungalows and stately Edwardian mansions.

Go under the bridge (Weybridge Road and buses 437, 461, 462 and 725) and follow the towpath as it curves to the right past a cottage. The line of the river which runs directly ahead is, in fact, the original River Wey while the Navigation, which we shall be following, turns sharp right. Thus the two routes diverge. At Byfleet they are a mile (1.6km) apart and it is not before another 6 miles (9.6km) that they join again near Newark Lock.

Continue to the path and turn left which brings you on to Addleston Road; the Navigation is directly ahead. This is Town Lock (unmanned) and you turn right along the towpath running along beside Addlestone Road, the water to your left. This is a most attractive straight channel, banked up on both sides and looking down upon the road. The technique of using the earth dug from the canal to form the banks is clearly shown here. Hamm Moor is over to the left. You will see notices referring to the different fishing sections through which we pass and that tickets are available from bailiffs. On some days fishing competitions are held and then the banks are lined with fishermen. At the next bridge (Black Boy Bridge) the path clearly goes onto the bridge and crosses over it onto the left bank. However, if you would like to call at The Pelican, an attractive waterside inn, do not go over the bridge just yet. Instead, follow the Addleston Road for just over 100yd (90m) and then turn first left into Hamm Moor Lane. The pub, set in lawns which run down to the river, is on your left.

Continuing from Black Boy Bridge we pass some of the very few industrial sites that we will meet on this walk. But just past the railway bridge we come to 'one of the best pieces of industrial architecture in Surrey', as Pevsner describes Coxes Mill. The main block is six storeys high but being surrounded by water it seems even higher. What is so startling is the windowless wall facing us which extends fully to the roof. Added to this there is the continuous roar from the weir which cascades down from the millpond. Coxes Mill began in the late eighteenth century as an iron foundry and mill, the water-race operating the machinery and a forging hammer. The earliest buildings are those beside the weir. It was not until the 1830s that it became a flour mill in which capacity it continued to operate until early 1983 when it was closed by Allied Mills. Until 1969 the grain was delivered to the mill by barge, and there was a brief revival of this method in 1981 before the final closure.

Grade II listing has been conferred on one eighteenth-century and two nineteenth-century structures which is tantamount to an overall listing. Until its closure Coxes Mill still contained some very old machinery of exceptional interest

Coxes Mill

and this will probably now be housed in a museum. The mill itself is earmarked for residential use which, these days, could promise something very special indeed. The highest buildings were constructed between 1901 and 1906 but look older, not so much Victorian as Georgian. The silos, however, are post-war. There are many details which make up this vigorous mass: the white loading-bay jutting out over the water; the disjunctive relationship of the buildings one to another; the hypnotic symmetry of lines of windows and the 'Manhattan' skyline.

Although this is a man-made stretch of the river it is, after hundreds of years, entirely naturalised and exceedingly beautiful. The millpond, to the right as we pass Coxes Lock, is as large as a lake! The Navigation continues in an almost straight line for nearly 2 miles (3.2km) and reference to a map would show how excessively contorted the old river is at this point.

The attractive houses on the right are on the New Haw Road while on the left is a pleasant donkey ranch. At the next bridge (Byfleet Road with buses 435, 436, 459, 725 and Byfleet railway station) you have to go over the road and down to the towpath which is, again, on the left side. To the right, along the bridge, is a shop and the White Hart pub. Nearby, to the east, is the world-famous Brooklands Racing Track which opened in 1907 with a circuit of nearly 3 miles (4.8km); its enormous width could take ten cars abreast. The last race was held in August 1939. During the war aircraft were built here and this began its use by British Aerospace which still owns the property. The prototype VC10 actually took off from the long straight section of the track.

Back on the towpath, and at New Haw Lock (where there is a slipway for launching boats) there is another clamorous weir; private boats are moored along the right bank for quite a way. The towpath now has a wonderful collection of trees: willows, alder and an avenue of oaks which are absolutely in their prime. We continue under the M25. Immediately past the M25 there is, on the right, one of the loveliest corners on our route: the entrance to the old Basingstoke Canal.

The canal has been derelict for years but it is now the subject of one of the most celebrated acts of restoration in the country.

It was opened in 1794 as part of an intended route to Southampton and the sea: a wonderful conception which would have given a direct link between two great ports, London and Southampton, and provided a shorter route than the long journey through the Straits of Dover. (It would have also avoided close contact with the French, which in the late eighteenth century was desirable.) But the scheme was never completed. The canal came to a dead-end, after 37 miles (59km), at Basingstoke and as it did not pass through any really productive industrial centres it did not prove to be commercially attractive. Construction costs were high, and the Canal company continually lost money. The coming of the London to Southampton railway in the 1830s was the death knell and, though it struggled on to 1866, the company finally closed. In 1966 the Surrey and Hampshire Canal Society was formed to restore the canal, and with the support of the county councils of Surrey and Hampshire and job creation grants, unexpected success has been achieved. This wonderful and beautiful river park, 24 miles (38km) long and with twenty-nine locks, will be opened once again, probably in the late 1980s.

After the railway bridge there is a delightful range of small houses on the right bank. This is a popular stretch for anglers and there are frequent competitions; from here to the next lock (Pyrford Lock) there can be as many as four hundred anglers. The cleaning up of London's rivers has been responsible for the extraordinary renaissance of fish life in these rivers. In the summer of 1983 history was made when the first Thames-spawned salmon was caught at Chertsey Lock. A splendid 7lb (3.15kg) specimen, it was given much publicity by the Thames Water Authority.

The old iron Parvis Bridge is very plain but it bears the early date of 1720. Here boats may be hired at the Byfleet Boat Club every weekend from Easter to September. The towpath leads onto the new bridge. Go diagonally left and pass along the left side of the cottage to rejoin the towpath. For shops and The Queen's Head pub you continue left along Parvis Road. Parvis Road is served by buses 437, 459, 730 and ¾ mile (1.2km) to the west (right) is West Byfleet railway station.

At the little timber footbridge (Murray's Bridge) the M25 mercifully curves away to the east, followed shortly afterwards by Dodd's Bridge. The watermeadows between the two bridges achieve a quite remarkably vivid green, even in a dry summer, which alternate with patches of dense growth on either bank. Just before the next bridge there is, to the right, Wisley Marina which was opened in 1983. It is a regular-shaped enclosure of water with a narrow entrance from the Navigation which offers safe moorings for privately owned boats.

Opposite the Marina is The Anchor pub where you can sit at tables in the garden which overlooks the water. Cross over Lock Lane and down onto the towpath beside Pyrford Lock. A number of houseboats are moored here; they include several of the enormous barges which used to use the Navigation and have now been converted. Pigeon House Bridge looks across luscious fields, cows grazing, and 1 mile (1.6km) or so over to the left are the famous gardens of the Royal Horticultural Society, Wisley, which are open to the public.

On the right is the private garden of Pyrford Place. We have a glimpse of a romantic corner beside the bank with, further

The summerhouse at Pyrford Place

on, a remarkable seventeenth-century summerhouse with a cupola-shaped roof. On the left is a small arm of the old River Wey which increases in size as we get nearer to the Walsham Flood Gates where the Navigation is some 12–15ft (3.6–4.5m) above the river. You will notice that Walsham Lock has, unusually, turf sides which is a pleasant change from the normal hard edge of stone or concrete. The towpath follows naturally across the tumultuous weir and we enter a new world: no actual towpath but the grassy banks of open English meadows, clusters of trees at their edges.

The gates at Newark Lock are dated 1970 and here it is important that you go over the lock and continue (until the next bridge) on the right bank. On the watermeadows (right) there stands the picturesque ruin of Newark Priory. Founded by Austin Canons in the late twelfth century, it grew into a flourishing monastic centre which, even the remains can tell us, must have created a remarkable and beautiful impression. Henry VIII closed it down and succeeding generations of builders and road-menders have robbed it of its stone, but for centuries it gave shelter to pilgrims tramping to Canterbury and the spirit of the place lives on.

At Newark Bridge go over the bridge and the towpath runs along the left bank. While crossing the bridge you can see the grand nineteenth-century Mill House which used to have an eighteenth-century wooden mill beside it, but the mill was unfortunately burnt down in 1966. Continuing along the towpath, the whole area is a maze of waterways – little cuts and hooks running in all directions often backing in upon themselves. Altogether the river fragments into seven different streams. At Paper Court Lock cross the lock to the right bank and proceed with the water on your left. However, just before the lock and the weir the old River Wey branches off to the right and in a series of over twenty sharp bends covers almost twice the distance of the Navigation before the two meet again at Worsfold Flood Gates.

The character now changes quite considerably. So overgrown is the path in places in summer, especially after Tanyard Bridge, where there are riverside works along the left bank, that one needs to be careful of nettles, brambles and even of

being edged into the water. If the small industrial estate buildings do not form the prettiest part of the walk they do at least
recall, with the waterside loading bays, the numerous similar
establishments that used to be a frequent sight in the past. At
High Bridge you can cross over to shops at Send village – just
five minutes' walk away.

At the next bridge, Cart Bridge and Broadmead Road, there
is the large New Inn. Buses 436 and 437 can be caught here;
Woking railway station, 2 miles (3.2km) to the west, is to the
right.

9 Send to Guildford
6 miles (9.5km)

Trains: Woking (British Rail)
Buses: 436, 437
Map: OS sheet no 186

From Woking railway station take bus 436 or 437 to Send. Alight at the New Inn. The towpath, a broad gravelled way, is to the right when you are facing the pub. You walk in a southerly direction with the water on your right.

At Worsfold Flood Gates the River Wey joins the Navigation after the type of circuitous route which made the Navigation such a boon to rivermen. Here also are the National Trust Workshops with many fine old barges moored alongside. On the left we are close to hilly country, part of the North Weald. Fields are stocked with sheep, horses and cattle.

At Triggs Lock the old river goes straight ahead so cross the small bridge and continue past the lock-keeper's cottage, a particularly lovely example dating from 1780. The towpath now follows the left bank of the Navigation. Here the Navigation has been banked up high and stands above the surrounding fields. The Navigation takes a long, slow sweep to the left, and across the fields, nestling among a line of trees, is St Mary's, Send. It dates from the thirteenth century but the battlemented tower, which is the part most visible to us, is in fifteenth-century Perpendicular style. Between us and the church the river winds unseen through the fields to rejoin the Navigation at a spectacular cataract further on.

Go over Send Church Bridge, which is on a line with the church, and the towpath now continues along the right bank. This bridge also leads to Sutton Place, but visits cannot be made without prior arrangement. We will not be able to see the house itself as it lies behind the trees which crowd upon the top of the hill. The Navigation was begun in 1650 by a former owner of Sutton Place, Sir Richard Weston. Sutton Place, the home of Paul Getty for many years, was an important sixteenth-century manor house; it also now contains a stupendous art collection.

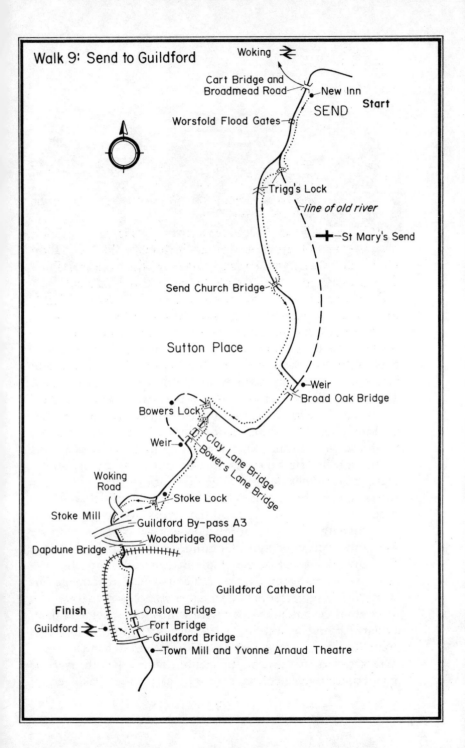

Walk 9: Send to Guildford

Woking

Cart Bridge and
Broadmead Road

New Inn

SEND

Start

Worsfold Flood Gates

Trigg's Lock

line of old river

St Mary's Send

Send Church Bridge

Sutton Place

Weir

Broad Oak Bridge

Bowers Lock

Weir

Clay Lane Bridge

Bowers Lane Bridge

Woking
Road

Stoke Lock

Stoke Mill

Guildford By-pass A3

Woodbridge Road

Dapdune Bridge

Guildford Cathedral

Finish

Guildford

Onslow Bridge

Fort Bridge

Guildford Bridge

Town Mill and Yvonne Arnaud Theatre

A typical small bridge across the River Wey

We come to the iron railings which line the private road to Sutton Place. Gradually the sound of the A3 becomes evident but that is soon obliterated by an enormous complex of weirs. Broad Oak Bridge, a high and sweeping arch, carries the road to Sutton Place and there are fine wrought-iron entrance gates. The towpath skirts the edge of a meadow which slopes down from the wooded hill, the water on your left. This is a short section of the original river with pleasant reedy banks, but we leave it at the next small bridge. The bridge (it might have a plank across it but that is only to keep out the cattle) crosses to a path where you turn left and then cross over Bowers Lock. The towpath is now on the left side and you continue with the Navigation on your right. Continue under Clay Lane Bridge then over the top of Bowers Lane Bridge down onto the towpath. The river is joined again on the right at a rather dangerous weir; for some reason that channel is not fenced off. The towpath is very richly grown with willow trees, some of them pollarded, and on the other side are open watery meadows with all along a thick growth of rushes. One feature of the Navigation is that, except for sections taken up with riverside properties, the banks have natural earth and grass verges, which means that over the centuries the Navigation has made its own interpretation of the shape of the banks, cutting out a little hollow here or adding something there to give man's work a very natural appearance. At Stoke Lock cross the new metal bridge and go to the lock and walk along the left bank. The view down to the old river gives a strong indication of the artificial construction of the Navigation as a good 15ft (4.5m) separate the height of the two waterways. You can see the line of trees that follows the old river sweeping in a curve to join the Navigation at Stoke Mill. This is an imposing Victorian mill of five storeys with different coloured bricks worked into the design. The towpath leads up onto the busy Woking Road (buses 285, 286 and 290) where you should cross straight over the road, turn left and then right at the end of the bridge's parapet. This brings you down once more to the towpath.

As you walk along the towpath look over to the left for a splendid view of Guildford's Cathedral of the Holy Spirit situated on the top of Stag Hill. It was designed in 1932 by Sir Edward Maufe who won the open competition, though building was interrupted by the war and its aftermath for twelve years and it was not consecrated until 1961. Guildford and Liverpool are the only cathedrals in England to be built on new sites since 1250.

We go under the Guildford Bypass, and at Woodbridge Road turn right, cross the road; the towpath is now running along the right bank. Over to the right is Walnut Tree Close, which is industrial in spite of its name, but a pleasant expanse of lawn gives privacy to the towpath. It is this industrial area, which had its last commercial delivery by water in 1969, that was the principal object of the old barges' journeys down the Navigation. Guildford was made prosperous by the Navigation which, in turn, sustained the waterways' transport industry.

After passing under the railway's Dapdune Bridge (1885) the towpath becomes a narrow track between a continuous wall and the bank. On the left can be seen the Dapdune Wharf with the new office (1968) of the National Trust. The wharf itself dates from the early nineteenth century and was the site of the boat-building yard of the Stevens family, the former owners of the Navigation who handed it over to the National Trust in

1964. The last barge was launched here in 1944, but building and the repair of pleasure craft continues.

Further along is the splendid Treadmill Crane, two hundred years old and capable of lifting up to a 3 ton load which it last did in 1908 when handling concrete building piles. It is here that the Wey Navigation officially ends and the Godalming Navigation begins. The Town Mill of 1766 now makes an interesting ensemble of styles with the adjacent Yvonne Arnaud Theatre (Scott, Brownrigg and Turner 1965), the mill now being used as the scenery workshop.

Return to Guildford Bridge where to the east side (same side as the theatre) there are many shops; the west side leads to the bus station and Guildford railway station.

HOGSMILL RIVER

Introduction

The Hogsmill is referred to as a river, stream or brook in different documents, records and books. Although its appearance resembles a stream over most of its length, it does take on the broader sweep of a river as it reaches Norbiton, and it enters the Thames at Kingston-upon-Thames with a final flourish; perhaps at this point 'river' is an acceptable title. But this very ambiguity is part of its attraction for there are few rivers which can give us, in the short distance of 6 miles (9.6km) or so, such a dramatic contrast from source to mouth as the Hogsmill. In turn it is, indeed, brook, stream and river.

It rises from a vigorous supply of water from springs at the centre of the old village of Ewell. This water, which is unusually cold, forms a delightful lake in the grounds of Bourne Hall and then runs in a north-westerly direction to the Thames. The village derives its name from this source as earlier spellings show: Etwell (ninth century) and Awell (twelfth century) really mean 'at the well'.

Archaeological remains have shown that there was a Roman settlement at Ewell. Possibly it was also on a Roman road from Sussex to the Thames and may have achieved some importance. The Domesday survey of 1086 records two watermills at Ewell so the industry which is part of the river's name had already begun by then. That a Mr Hogge once owned a mill on the river which then adopted his name may be purely circumstantial but there is no firm origin otherwise for the river's name. However, there is no doubt that watermills existed in considerable numbers. The grinding of the ingredients of gunpowder was an early and important industry in Surrey and the Hogsmill was mentioned in the licence awarded in 1588 to the father and son, George and John Evelyn. Gunpowder-making later transferred to Chilworth near Guildford but flour-mills continued to use waterpower from the Hogsmill until the nineteenth century.

The driving power of the river, as will be seen, is not very great today but it was very much stronger in earlier times. Then the river had a number of small streams flowing into it from Epsom and Ashstead Commons which, added to the springs, gave it its industrial strength. It was during the eighteenth century that clay-working on the commons in the manufacture of bricks, and increased ploughing as more land was taken up for agriculture, caused the delicate balances of water supply to the Hogsmill to be affected. This diminishing waterpower was eventually to affect the cloth-working trade at Kingston which had to close down because of it. Indeed, it was navigable to some extent in former times and a scheme was even considered to canalise it, but now the strength and depth are no more and it is, for the most part, just a lovely, rural backwater.

There are still two mills at Ewell although their commercial days have long since passed. The Lower Mill has been converted to offices and outwardly remains a fine example of Georgian architecture, but the Upper Mill still exists in much of its original state. However, like the hotly fought battle in 1958 to save Ewell's Tudor cottages, the Friends of the Mill are trying to ward off an enervating 'tasteful' conversion to a pub.

The rural nature of the river is remarkable. Its route is through some heavily urbanised stretches but the prolific growth of trees which shield nearly all the housing from view creates a feeling of privacy. When the river does lose this cover, as when it approaches Villiers Road at Kingston, then the thrill of the hunt becomes the attraction as we trace the route from one street to another. To reach the point where the Hogsmill flows into the Thames is both exciting and fulfilling.

There are two places were you are forced to leave the river because of a depot in Worcester Park Road and the Sewage Works at Lower Marsh Lane. However, there is a plan under consideration to open up the riverside walk in these places.

96

10   Ewell West to Kingston-upon-Thames
6 miles (9.6km)

Trains: Ewell West (British Rail)
Buses: 293; London Country 406, 408, 468, 472, 476;
      Green Line 727
Map: OS sheet no 176

From Ewell West station turn left at the road (Chessington
Road) and where it divides turn right into Spring Road – named
after the source of the Hogsmill. The road curves to the left and
on the left will be seen Bourne Hall, a modern, circular building housing the public library. On entering the forecourt, follow the low wall on your right and pass through the entrance
into the park where you almost immediately bear right. This
brings you to the grand main gate arch (entrance to the old
Bourne Hall) adorned with animal sculptures, and to the lodge
house, all in brilliant white. To the left is a delightful lake.
Here, with the spring water issuing from culverts beneath our
feet, is the source of the Hogsmill River.

    Going away from the arch and with the water on your right,

The Upper Mill, Ewell

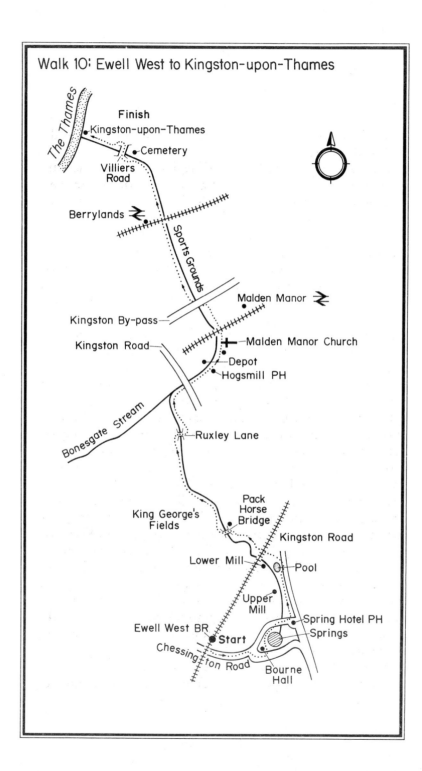

Walk 10: Ewell West to Kingston-upon-Thames

The Thames

Finish
Kingston-upon-Thames

Cemetery

Villiers
Road

Berrylands

Sports Grounds

Malden Manor

Kingston By-pass

Kingston Road

Malden Manor Church

Depot

Hogsmill PH

Bonesgate Stream

Ruxley Lane

Pack
Horse
Bridge

King George's
Fields

Kingston Road

Lower Mill

Pool

Upper
Mill

Spring Hotel PH

Ewell West BR

Springs

Start

Chessington Road

Bourne
Hall

follow the lake around. Up to the left you will see the new Bourne Hall completed in the early 1970s to a design by Sheppard Fidler. Looking up the slope of a green lawn this strange finned 'spaceship' appears to be rising slowly over the top of the hill. The old hall of 1775 was last used as a girls school before it was vacated and left to run down. It was demolished in 1970.

The lakeside path leads on to Chessington Road where the river walk continues to the right across the road. From there you can see, further right still, the Spring Hotel which is an old inn at the junction of the Kingston and London roads. Very soon we come to the Upper Mill: magnificent industrial architecture from the early nineteenth century, towering, weatherboarded and gabled. There are records of a mill having been on this site from the tenth century. Crossing by the bridge to the front of the mill, you can see a millstream which was cut to supply power for the mill but formerly it would have had a considerably greater flow. What we have now are the buildings of the mill itself but until recently there was an adjoining early eighteenth-century mill house. It was unfortunately burnt down and part of the argument against the case for restoring the mill is that half of the original buildings have now been lost.

Continue along the path to the right of the river. It leads out onto the pavement of Kingston Road for here the river opens out into a very wide pool, an exotic water space of reeds, lilies and willow trees. On the right is the Eight Bells and coming up on the left is the eighteenth-century Lower Mill. It was originally a flour mill then a paper mill and now comprises offices. The siting of the mill beside the river has prevented the walk continuing along its bank. Therefore we have to carry on straight ahead along Meadow Walk. Go under the railway bridge and immediately turn left along a pathway which runs between the railway embankment (left) and a small house (right). Lower down you come once more to the Hogsmill. Do not cross the footbridge but keep to the right bank. Here the stream is very small. At certain times of the year it is almost obliterated by some rather splendid watercress.

We pass through a pleasant open park, the river running at the bottom of a distinct valley. There are a great number of hawthorn trees, grassy meadows and a firm gravel path. We come to a conjunction with a stream (left) which rises out of Epsom Common: one of the streams which formerly gave the Hogsmill greater waterpower. Although there are houses bordering the park on either side, you can scarcely see them because they are all fronted by groves of trees. We leave the watercress behind and the river assumes that lovely clarity which made it such an excellent supplier in earlier times of trout for the London market. This was one of the most important trades which could be carried on on most of the small tributaries of the Thames. The willow trees which now begin to assume such billowing proportions, linking branches across the water, will be a continuing delight almost to the end of the walk.

After passing a set of stepping stones (do not cross them), we enter a wood which closes in upon us in contrast to the previous open spaces; the willows here are among the tallest you are likely to see. We reach a wire-fence enclosure. Keep left and work your way over a little sluice, up a small hillock and down again to the river. On reaching a small concrete bridge make a short detour to the right where, after 20yd (18m), you can see across a field to an attractive and ancient packhorse bridge that used to carry a road to Kingston. Steeply humped and in that warm eighteenth-century brick, it stands isolated in its field, a nostalgic reminder of a previous highway. Return to the concrete bridge. Cross over and take the path along the left bank, with the water to your right, going past a small weir. There is a firm, new path, King George's Fields over to the left and benches to sit on. Another little stream leads in from the right, which rises in the lake at Ewell Court Hall. We pass by another footbridge at Oakland Way – the river lies secretly between narrow, deep banks filled with reeds. To the right is one of the many plantations of trees which have been established with oak, birch, willow, lime and poplar.

At the next footbridge, where Alway Road (left) curves down towards us, cross the footbridge and follow along the right bank of the river to Ruxley Lane. There was a ford here known as Ruxley Splash and as this was the only road in Ewell across the Hogsmill it was a well-known and busy crossing point. Another little stream joins from the left just as we reach the bridge. Cross the road and the path is straight ahead. It is a surfaced path but where it bends to the right after about 80yd (72m) keep straight ahead going on to an earth track. This is a pleasantly urban stretch: dogs out for their walks, kids in prams, housewives doing the shopping and small boys' tireless feet keeping down the weeds. It is good to see that the river is not purely recreational and that people can work it into their daily activities.

Ahead you will see some powerlines and, joining on the left, is a stream that used to be an important contributor to the Hogsmill's water supply. It is the Bonesgate Stream which rises from Ashtead Common, flows through Chessington and joins the Hogsmill here just south of the Kingston Road. The Bonesgate flows through land which is still mainly used for agriculture. The Hogsmill does nearly a right-angle turn to the Kingston Road. Cross the road and slightly over to the right is Worcester Park Road. The river is to your left but keep to the pavement for 80yd (72m). On drawing level with the first house on your right, take the track left through the trees and towards the river.

The course of the river is now very straight, the trees forming quite a thick wood of youngish growth. The great Victorian painters, John Millais and Holman Hunt, often used the Hogsmill for background scenery. It is said that Holman Hunt, who lived in Worcester Park, used as a model for the cottage door at which Christ is knocking in the famous painting 'The Light of the World' one of the many small buildings at the gunpowder factory which was here at the time. On reaching the small bridge, have a look along the river from the unusual bays built into the iron railings; they were designed for refuge from passing carts. Because of a depot beside the river the route now continues along the pavement for just over half a mile. The Hogsmill pub, which is over on the other side of the road, serves a wide range of food. It stands on the site of a former mill.

The name of the road becomes Malden Lane, then Church Road passing (left) a charming weatherboard cottage 'The Lodge' and further on (again left) two splendid Victorian

101

'Tudor' houses of 1879. Then, turning left into a little unsurfaced lane, you come to the manor house, the parish church of St John the Baptist and farm buildings of Old Malden. For such an unassuming setting this group of buildings has had an eventful history.

The church is of Saxon origin and it is probably original flintwork that can be seen at the east end. The Saxon description 'Mael Dune' (Cross on the hill) is, of course, now Malden and refers to the slope down to the Hogsmill. The manor house stands behind the high wall just before reaching the church; the present house is a lovely Queen Anne building from about 1700. In 1240 the manor became the property of Walter de Merton, a clerk at the great Priory nearby at Merton. In 1261 he became Chancellor of England though he was deposed during the Barons' Revolt of Simon de Montfort and the manor was ransacked (1264). Walter established Merton College at Oxford in 1264, and at first it was administered from the manor. In the sixteenth century, Henry VIII took land from the parish to add to his amazing Nonsuch Palace; Commissioners appointed by Edward VI took away practically everything from the church that could be moved (1553); in 1578 Elizabeth I brought great pressure to bear upon Merton College to give up the estate but it was restored to the college forty years later. The living of St John's and the freehold of much of the surrounding land is still held by Merton College to this day. Not surprisingly, the buildings suffered and the church shows clearly the evidence of rebuilding. Most remarkable is the Jacobean tower (1610) which is so plain and functional that it could be twentieth century. The church is usually open and should not be missed.

Continue along the lane past Victorian farm buildings (right) with the date 1855 worked into the gable in coloured bricks, and two small cottages also owned by Merton College. The path slopes down to the Hogsmill; do not cross the footbridge but keep to the broad main path along the right bank and go under the railway bridge. For Malden Manor railway station turn right. Continue past the school playing fields (right) and through grassy paddocks separated by dense clusters of hawthorn.

This leads directly up onto the Kingston Bypass where you have to turn left for 200yd (180m) to the subway (where there are shops and buses 72 and 152) and cross under the road to return (right) to the river. It is clearly signposted 'Hogsmill Walk'. On meeting another small tributary coming in from the left, you have to turn left and follow it to the road (Elmbridge Avenue). Here you turn right but do not rejoin the river; instead we have another detour. Turn left into Surbiton Hill Park, second right (Chiltern Drive) and then under the railway bridge at Berrylands railway station. This brings you onto Lower Marsh Lane (the sewage works over the wall to the right has closed the river route) and then 500yd (450m) further on, to Villiers Road where you turn right. The Hogsmill is reached again, after 200yd (180m), at the bridge. Here (right) there is an attractive new industrial development along the river, the most important feature for ourselves being the new river walk which has clearly been required for building consent. It ends at the grounds of Kingston Cemetery.

Cross straight over Villiers Road to the river where it emerges from under the bridge. It is about 35ft (10m) wide and flowing briskly between enclosed banks. Turn right (north) up Villiers Road where, just before reaching a depot of tall storage tanks, you turn left along a small path. This is where we begin a completely different part of our walk as we track the Hogsmill through the streets of Kingston on its way to the Thames.

Just after our path returns to the Hogsmill we come to The Swan pub (Mill Street) where the path now goes over a small bridge to the left side of the river. This brings us to a fine conjunction with an old millstream, the widest part of the Hogsmill along its entire course. On the right Kingston Polytechnic has some attractive new buildings which make a fine river frontage. Continue on to Portland Road and turn right passing Myrtle Cottages, characteristic nineteenth-century artisans' dwellings. Turn right at Springfield Road for a splendid view of the river and the Polytechnic. Retrace your steps, then cross Springfield Road to Denmark Street where, just past the carpark (right), there is a narrow path leading to the Hogsmill with a view of two weirs from the footbridge. Return to the road and turn right. Cross over the main road (Penrhyn

Road), turn right and then take the left fork into St James's Road. On the left are the new buildings of the Guildhall (Roy Roe 1981) where the gravel path clearly leads down to the Hogsmill. Further on is the superb twelfth-century Clattern Bridge, one of the oldest bridges in Surrey and a scheduled ancient monument. Here a small gate at the north-west corner of the bridge leads to a short platform where the original piers and the three arches of the bridge can be seen. You will also see, for the first time, boats moored on the river. Return to the gate, turn right towards the bingo hall and then right into the unnamed road which runs along the side of the hall. From the carpark on the right there is a good view of the Hogsmill from steps which lead down to the water – we are within 80yd (72m) of our goal.

By continuing to the end of the road we reach the Thames. On the right is a small houseboat community where, by asking permission of a resident, you might cross over several gang planks to reach journey's end at the mouth of the Hogsmill River: we are about 450yd (405m) above Kingston Bridge.

Return to the bingo hall and go left to the Clattern Bridge. Have a look at the Coronation Stone signposted in front of the Guildhall (Maurice Webb 1935) upon which seven Saxon kings were crowned in the Saxon Chapel of St Mary's Church between 900 and 979: note the seven-sided railings to this monument. Return to the road and continue ahead to the Market Place; keep to the left side of the road. Where the line of shop fronts suddenly opens out into the square of Market Place, turn left down King's Passage to The Gazebo pub, a fine position on the waterfront with pavilions on either side of river stairs. These were formerly the water-stairs to the tea garden of Nuttall's Restaurant; we will see the grand old façade when we return to the square. The pub, built in a traditional design, was opened in the summer of 1982 but the two pavilions, or gazebos, are the original ones built for the restaurant. The pub's interior reflects modern enthusiasm for the antique.

Return to the Market Place. The Town Hall (1840), with corner towers, is by Charles Henman and the first-floor statue of Queen Anne (1700) is by the outstanding English sculptor Francis Bird. The spectacular gabled premises, now occupied by Millets, was formerly the famous Nuttall's Restaurant.

Continue in the northerly direction along Thames Street and turn right at the main road, Clarence Street. Pass the parish church of All Saints (right). The road curves round into Eden Street with the bus station on the right and on to Kingston railway station (left).

THREE SUBURBAN BROOKS

Introduction

This group of walks takes us through busy residential and commercial areas of North London yet passes through glades and rolling downs with a variety which rivals Surrey's. Access is easy from a multitude of points. It lies within a network of main roads for car users and there are plenty of bus routes and underground stations en route.

The Dollis Brook is the principal stream changing its name to the River Brent as it nears the North Circular Road and flows west through the Welsh Harp Reservoir, also known as the Brent Reservoir. This was created in the 1830s by damming up the River Brent and using the ensuing large lake as a feeder to the Grand Union Canal to help maintain the canal's level of water. Named after a pub which stood nearby, the Welsh Harp became a popular pleasure spot during the latter part of the nineteenth century and retains its popularity today as a centre for water sports. The River Brent runs from the North Circular Road to Brentford where it then joins the Thames. Folly Brook and Mutton Brook are tributaries of the Dollis Brook.

Two ridges of high land running east to west, Totteridge and The Ridgeway, are the watersheds which give rise to the Dollis and Folly Brooks. Mutton Brook rises from the western slopes of Muswell Hill and Highgate and joins the Dollis near the North Circular Road at the junction with the Brent River. Moat Mount Recreation Ground (western end of Totteridge Lane) covers an area which gives rise not only to the Dollis and Folly Brooks but also swells another network, more to the west, which centres upon Dean's Brook and the Silk Stream, the latter also flowing into the Welsh Harp. Most of the Dollis, Mutton and Folly Brooks are accessible to walkers. The Dollis is a particularly comfortable walk, even with babes in prams, for most of the path has been surfaced with asphalt.

East Finchley, where our walk begins, has a good old Saxon name meaning 'wood with finches'. Formerly known as East End, it was one of the gates to the Bishop of London's Park which he allowed travellers to use as a direct route to and from London. The tolls were collected at the tollgate on the hill, ie Highgate, but were discontinued at the beginning of the nineteenth century. Dick Turpin is alleged to have jumped this gate on his horse Black Bess when riding to York.

Once the traveller continued north from East End he could be prey to the most avaricious collectors, the highwaymen of Finchley Common, one of the most desolate and dangerous areas in the vicinity of London. A great number of coaches and horse riders used to pass this way; a hundred and fifty coaches a day would pull into the staging-post at Barnet. Lucrative swag was also to be picked up from the farmers returning from the cattle market at Smithfield after driving their cattle over Finchley Common and through Highgate and Islington.

The common was indeed a versatile place. Cattle were grazed (eg Mutton Brook), hunting took place in the forest, horse-races and boxing matches were held, executions were carried out, armies gathered and were trained, a famous hog market flourished and refugees from the plagues fled from the City to the clear air of the common. With the Inclosure Act of 1814 the common was brought under control and the high-waymen were finally put out of business: we may now commence our walk in safety.

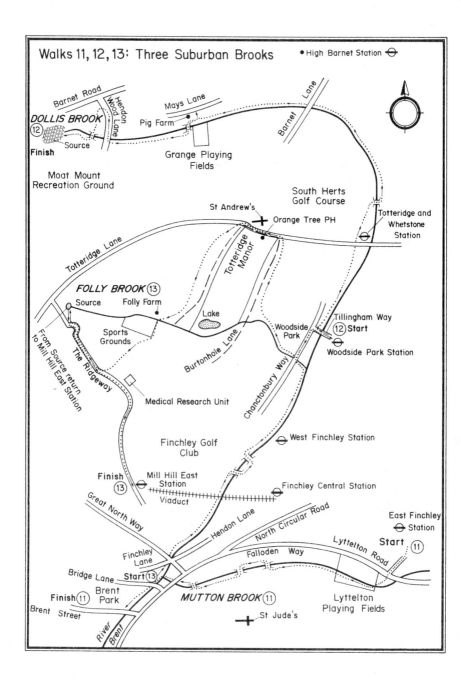

Walks 11, 12, 13: Three Suburban Brooks

● High Barnet Station

11   Mutton Brook to Brent Park
2½ miles (4km)

Trains: East Finchley underground station
Bus: 102, 104, 143, 263
Map: OS sheet no 176

From East Finchley station turn immediately right and right
again going under the railway bridge. Take the first right (The
Bishop's Avenue), another right (Deansway), then first left
(Vivian Way) where the Mutton Brook flows behind the
crescent of houses on the left side. Cross straight over
Lyttelton Road (bus 102), under which the brook flows.
Slightly to the right is Norrice Lea where, between houses Nos
16 and 18, you enter Lyttelton Playing Fields. Follow the path
round, turning right between the pavilion and the tennis
courts. Here we meet the Mutton Brook (right). It is about 7ft
(2m) wide with its banks supported by wooden planks. The
playing fields are spacious and rise on the left over to
Hampstead Garden Suburb. This 'ideal' community was
begun in 1907 as the idea of Dame Henrietta Barnett. Traditional English building styles were adopted ranging from the
artisan's cottage to middle-class villas and expensive mansions
in the Georgian style. Pubs and shops were excluded but crafts
and community activities were encouraged especially in
Central Square where the Institute and two churches, all by
Lutyens, were intended to be a gathering point. To the south-
east the robust spire of one of these churches, Lutyen's great St
Jude's Church (1910) dominates the skyline. Follow over the
brick bridge and after a pleasantly wooded section and a
wooden bridge we come to Kingsley Way.
   From the road bridge there is a beautiful view ahead of an
ornamental garden. The calm, level lawns, the brook, the
freely shaped flower beds and the seemingly random planting
of silver birches and shrubs have the studied naturalism of a
Japanese garden. The path continues between wooden railings,
and there is access to this garden, appropriately called a 'Quiet
Garden', at the end of the path.
   Cross straight over Northway and enter Northway Gardens

where there are tennis courts, a putting green and toilets. The path follows directly beside the brook which is lined by a fine avenue of willows. Cross over the path which leads down from Midholm and eventually arrive at Falloden Way.

At this point the brook goes under the road to emerge in a pretty little wild place before turning back to its normal course. You can follow it around, but for a more direct route turn left on reaching Falloden Way and continue ahead along Addison Way. Take the first turning on the right which is a small path that runs down to rejoin the brook; turn left. This is a most attractive section with the land sloping down from either side of the brook to form a miniature valley. From the vantage point at the next little bridge we can see the brook entering the tunnel which takes it under the Finchley Road. Cross the road and the path continues ahead behind the famous garage known as Henlys Corner (buses 13, 26, 102, 260).

The valley continues and high above us is the traffic of the North Circular Road. This monster circulatory system, begun in the 1930s, is a hotch-potch of purpose-built sections and old traditional routes which frequently results in traffic jams. This section, from Chiswick to Southgate, was constructed as an arterial road and more often than not behaves like one. Down by the brook, however, is one of the densest copses of willows that we shall see.

The path follows the brook through a spacious tunnel under the North Circular Road, from which there are access points. Shortly after this the Mutton Brook comes to its end when it flows into the main Dollis-Brent stream. At this intersection the path comes to a T-junction where the left turn along the Brent River takes us into Brent Park. The right turn leads us to the walk along the Dollis Brook which is detailed in the next section (Walk 12).

Turning left, therefore, over the small bridge leads to Bridge Lane where the entrance to Brent Park is across to the left. On entering the park take the path which bears around to the right and takes you between the Brent River (right) and a large pond. The park, which runs along one side of the North Circular Road, is ½ mile (0.8km) long and quite narrow. From the open valley of the previous part of the walk this park contains a wealth of tall trees which form an overhead canopy in summer-time.

Follow the path over a bridge and turn right. Towards the end of the park bear right over a wooden bridge and follow the river as it makes its way through the grounds of a new estate. Just before Brent Street the river broadens out to flow over an attractive rock-strewn weir with, either side, round, pointed 'medieval' towers standing guard. By crossing the road to the other side of the bridge the Brent can be seen to be about 50ft (15m) wide but without a path on either bank.

The walk from Lyttelton Playing Fields to Brent Park has followed a busy main road; nevertheless, the succession of parks and open spaces has given a sense of natural habitat far greater than might be expected. But for the river this urban countryside would have long since been destroyed. (Buses at Brent Street 83, 183, 240.)

12 Dollis Brook to Grange Playing Fields (or source)
5 miles (8km) or 7 miles (11.2km)

Trains: There is no convenient station at this point
Buses: 112, 182; Green Line 732, 743 (alight at Bridge Lane)
Map: OS sheet no 176

We will take up this walk exactly at the place where we turned at the T-junction in the preceding walk (Walk 11) to follow the small stretch of the Brent River, although a number of alternative starting places are given during the description.

From Bridge Lane (off the North Circular Road) turn on to the river (due north) and continue for a few yards where you cross a small bridge; the Mutton Brook flows in from the right but our route is directly ahead. Almost immediately the Dollis takes on its characteristic winding course, a feature that will predominate right to its source. We soon pass under the Great North Way (no access) and then come to an imposing weir at Hendon Lane (bus 143). Here it is better to avoid the dreadful underpass and cross the road where (right) we can reach the path again.

Hendon Lane leads to the small enclave (left 12 minutes) of St Mary's parish church and Church Farm House which are seventeenth-century remains of the old village, but the noble aerodrome with its famous air displays (1920–37) is no more. Memories of Handley Page, De Havilland and Grahame White are kept alive in the RAF Museum.

Having crossed Hendon Lane, the path winds through a rich forest of trees which forms quite a bird sanctuary. Shortly after crossing Waverley Grove the parkland opens out into a saucer-shaped area suggesting the rolling downs which we shall meet later on. This is Windsor Open Space; there are swings and see-saws and access points from a number of roads running from Hendon Lane and Holders Hill.

When we reach a T-junction it will be easily recognised; sports fields ahead, a long, narrow path (right) running uphill to Finchley Church End and, left, a small bridge which we cross, then turn immediately right. On reaching the road

(Dollis Road), turn right and go towards the great Mill Hill Viaduct. It was built in 1867 for the London North Eastern Railway's branch line to Mill Hill. This was a busy steam-train service carrying city workers to Liverpool Street Station. It is one of the most spectacular works of railway architecture in south-east England and is built with a particularly fine tone of red brick. The thirteen vast, slender arches are as impressive when viewing them lengthways from under the viaduct as when approaching them from a distance. By 1941 the line had been electrified by London Transport and became part of the extensive Northern line. Until axed by Beeching, locomotives continued to thunder through the little Finchley Central Station. The single stop from Finchley Central to Mill Hill by tube is well worth the short journey just for the panoramic views.

Continue along Dollis Road and go under the viaduct, but at the corner where the road bends to the right (for Finchley Central station and buses 13, 26, 260) carry straight on towards the trees. Here you meet the Dollis once again at a small foot-bridge which you go over. The path winds through a glade secluded amid trees with Finchley Golf Course to the left.

When you come to the next bridge, a brick one, you will see that it is approached from the other side by an avenue of gigantic chestnut trees, a continuation of Eversleigh Road. This avenue was formerly a private road to Nether Court (1883) which is now the club house of Finchley Golf Course. The course retains the original landscaping of the old grounds which rise picturesquely towards Mill Hill, an exceptionally beautiful setting for the sport.

Now cross the brick bridge and take the path first left which curves round and goes over a wooden footbridge. Should the ground be dry enough, however, there is a delightful small lake to explore in the area between the last two bridges; it is rich in birdlife and has a small island at its centre.

Once over the wooden bridge the path continues past an arched 'Japanese' bridge (a continuation of Lovers Walk) where, to the left, is a path for a short detour to Nether Court. From the Japanese bridge the river winds most attractively through steep banks, indicating the scourging of flood waters, and leads to Fursby Avenue (West Finchley station right) which you cross over and enter Woodside Park. This is a pleasantly landscaped park, long and narrow, with the path taking a broad sweep past the river's convolutions. We pass tennis courts (a small path leads in from Westbury Road) and reach Lullington Garth. With so many access points it can be seen that the walk may be picked up at a number of places.

Cross over Lullington Garth and continue on through the next section of Woodside Park. At the point where the path turns left you will see that this is where the Folly Brook, flowing in from the left, joins the Dollis. On reaching Chanctonbury Way we are at a place which we shall pick up again on our walk along the Folly Brook (see Walk 13). For the present, however, turn right at Chanctonbury Way and take the first right (Tillingham Way) where we join the Dollis (left) once more. (Continuing along Tillingham Way brings you to Woodside Park station.) This section, which runs along a narrow strip between the very winding brook and football fields, can be very muddy in wet weather so stout shoes are necessary.

Cross Laurel Walk Road and join Riverside Walk through a much more spacious park; then go over a small bridge to the east side of the brook. This is a very spectacular section. We can see quite clearly the scooped-out shape of the Brent Valley as the ground rises left and right to Longland Drive (left) and Ridgeview Road.

We now come to Totteridge Lane much of which, together with the Common and Totteridge Village, is designated as a conservation area. (Totteridge and Whetstone station; bus 251 and, nearby, buses 26, 34, 125, 134, 263.) The name Totteridge is very old indeed and might even have Saxon origins; 'tot' meant a small wood. 'Wooded ridge' is appropriate even today as Totteridge has retained much of its old, rural character. The fine views from the ridge have always attracted people with means, and a walk along the Lane reveals old and substantial properties; but the most endearing quality of Totteridge is its gentle, rural informality which gives it an entirely English charm.

Cross Totteridge Lane and the path is just over to the left. It begins as a narrow, grassy track before opening out into a park. The very marked shape of the valley continues rising up quite high to Whetstone (right) which used to be an important coaching and horse-breeding centre. Ahead the tall white building is Northway House. The path goes past a cluster of football fields, and leads across the brook towards a large pavilion; turn left at the T-junction. An access to this area is along the path opposite Buckingham Avenue (High Road, Whetstone) which brings you to the pavilion.

This begins the grandest section of the brook. We pass South Herts Golf Course (left) rising in great sweeps up the hill with the Dollis Brook, in the valley, winding, as ever, deeply between its tree-lined banks. Where previously the brook has gone through intimate, at times secluded, settings now it is all spacious and grand. Later, where the path divides, bear left towards the end of the terrace of houses (Western Way) which is ahead. The path crosses the cul-de-sac end of Western Way, and just a little further on turn left at the T-junction. There is a splendid view right up the hill to High Barnet.

Barnet is probably a name of Saxon origin meaning a clearing burnt out of the woods, the great forests of Middlesex. It was the scene of a famous battle of the Wars of the Roses in 1474; and Charles I escaped to Barnet when fleeing to Oxford during the Civil War. Elizabeth I would pass through Barnet when going to her great house at Hatfield. Our path crosses over Barnet Lane (right for High Barnet station, buses 34, 84, 107, 134, 263 and The Old Red Lion) where it continues with the made-up surface.

Now we have come to the top of the 'downs'. We have walked along the valley, but now the higher, rolling land falls away to the hollow of the Dollis Brook below. The views are quite superb for we are going along part of the southern face of the Hertfordshire Hills. The brook's winding course becomes yet more compressed as we follow it nearer to its source. There is an attractive new estate to the right but otherwise the view is unobstructed at three points of the compass and extends to the horizon of tree-topped hills.

A path comes in (right) from Leeside giving access from Mays Lane (bus 26) or from Wood Street (bus 107) via Manor

The Dollis Brook, nestling within the Hertfordshire hills

Road. The path then runs along Dollis Brook Walk but you leave the road at the small roundabout and bear left across the grass; we are again walking parallel to the brook (left). Do not cross the bridge (left) but keep straight ahead and go through an opening in the fence crossing over what is often an exceedingly muddy lane. We pass through Grange Playing Fields, the brook now getting very narrow but the water as clear as ever as it runs over a gravel bed.

The route ahead is blocked by a hedge and there are the splendid country aromas of a pig farm. There are now several possible routes. You can turn right at the hedge and go to Mays Lane (bus 26) or go left over the bridge and stile in the direction of the signpost to Totteridge Lane (bus 251). But for the intrepid walker who wishes to explore the brook further, cross the stile and turn right. From now on it is a matter of negotiating your way along the bank of the brook (right). Several tracks are crossed which lead to Mays Lane (right), as well as crossing playing fields which also lead to Mays Lane. The character of the brook now changes as it reaches its source for periodically it floods into broad watermeads full of willows and tufted grass.

Hendon Wood Lane now cuts across the Dollis, and to reach the source it is necessary to turn right along this road. Go up the hill and just before the T-junction with Barnet Road (bus 107) there is a public footpath (left) to Mill Hill. The sign to the footpath may be difficult to find as it is embedded within a holly tree, but it can be located by the names of two houses: Tree Lodge is next to the sign and Oak House is opposite on the other side of the road.

The path runs between wooden fences. When the fence on the left turns left, follow it around (going south). This leads through a grove of trees which ends at a grassy field. Cross straight over this field down to the Dollis which runs below. On reaching the brook turn right (water on your left) and turn left when you reach a stile sited next to a sizeable pond. Cross the stile (Mill Hill straight ahead) and turn almost immediately right. We are now walking up rising ground, the brook to the right, and this takes us up the watershed and source of the Dollis.

At the second field gate (right) we come to the end of our walk for the damp ground which surrounds us (in wet weather there are sheets of water on the ground) is the source which drains into the tree-lined channel of the Dollis Brook and continues till it joins the Thames at Brentford. For the return, retrace your steps to the stile. Cross over it and continue to retrace your route back to Hendon Wood Lane where you turn left. A short distance further on you reach Barnet Road and bus 107, which also takes you to High Barnet underground station.

13 Folly Brook to The Ridgeway (or source)
3 miles (4.8km)

Trains: Woodside Park underground station
Buses: 26, 125, 263
Map: OS sheet no 176

Woodside Park station, though now on the Northern line, was originally served by steam trains. It is an exceptionally pretty station. It was restored in 1974 by The Finchley Society, a restoration which revealed the delightful, creamy tone of its white Suffolk brick.

Leave the station by the northbound exit. Turn right at Holden Road and first left into Tillingham Way. Here we cross over the Dollis Brook before turning left at the T-junction with Southover. On reaching the open space, turn right into Woodside Park with spacious meadows extending northwards up from the brook (right). It can be very wet here, especially after rain. Many birds can be seen among the dense groves of trees. The path is not made up, just running along a grassy track.

Cross over a stile and along the foot of a large field rising over to the north-west, typical of Hertfordshire landscape. There are lots of willow trees growing thickly in the water of the Folly Brook. Also nearby are great elms and oak trees, a beautifully wooded landscape. We follow a worn track over the field while the brook does a huge loop.

Our track takes us over a small feeder stream running into the Folly which then curves away to the right. Ahead various worn tracks take us up and over beautiful heathland. From the top there are airy, spacious views, the horizon completely wooded. East to the perimeter of Woodside Park, only roof-tops show amid the trees; to the south-west is the tree-lined summit of Mill Hill and The Ridgeway; and north are all the fine things at Totteridge: the manor lands, the village and the 'ridge'. Down below the Folly rambles along amid willows.

We now arrive at Burtonhole Lane, or rather a country track which extends from it. Here we turn right, cross the book and go uphill towards Totteridge Green. Over the brook the extensive open countryside to the left is under the care of the

Totteridge Manor Association and was the demesne of the old manor. This delightfully rural lane is ideal for short walks between the two ridges of Totteridge and Mill Hill. It is visually delightful in both directions.

Continuing up the lane northwards we are, of course, leaving the brook behind us to continue its westward course. We are unable to follow it at this point because of the heavily fenced properties which close it off. However, we shall make a detour around the old demesne to pick up the brook again further on. In the meantime we shall have the opportunity to enjoy some of the delights of Totteridge village.

A fence appears to bar our progress along the lane but to the left you will see that parallel bars will enable you to continue along a small footpath. A wooden board stating 'footpath' may be nailed up on a tree. After mounting a stile the path emerges at Totteridge Green where we turn left (north). This is a spot of considerable charm. There is the traditional pond well stocked with ducks and geese, old farm buildings and a small close of picturesque housing. Then continue north to Totteridge Lane (bus 251) and turn left. This takes us through the old village and past a number of delightful houses. In 1968 this was designated a conservation area.

On the left we pass the celebrated Orange Tree pub and its pond. Further on there is the parish church of St Andrews (right) which had a long association with the Pepys family. The presence of the mighty thousand-year-old yew tree which stands in front of the church suggests a foundation of great antiquity. The present church dates from the late eighteenth century, although the wooden bell-turret, a nice piece of country carpenter's work, dates from 1706 and was retained from the previous church. To the left of the church stands a magnificent black barn. A small fenced area in front of it is the traditional site, from the late sixteenth century, of the old village pond.

Directly opposite the church is a footpath to Mill Hill which is entered just past the large gateway to The Darlands. The path runs downhill – we are descending to the Folly Brook again – and eventually goes between picket fences. When the going levels out we are passing (left) Darlands Nature Reserve with, amid this lightly forested area, Totteridge Ornamental Waters.

At the stile we go diagonally across a field. Even though planted with a crop, we are asked to keep to this bisecting route. At the far corner we cross another stile and join the Folly Brook. The route follows a very narrow path between brook and a wooden fence, a lovely little walk amid plenty of trees with land rising to either side.

The path leads on to a wider lane with a new house (right) on the site of the old Folly Farm. It is an attractive house with the interesting combination of a traditional vernacular weatherboarded front and a modern glass structure. Turn left and almost immediately right, skirting the edge of a playing field and passing the pretty old farm pond.

Deposited on the hill to the left is the vast bulk of Maxwell Ayrton's National Institute for Medical Research (1939) with its green copper roof. Its work on the common cold is its most publicised activity. Follow along the line of the brook, over a small bridge, and enter another playing field. By keeping the Folly on your right you arrive at a line of trees and a small rivulet where you have two choices: either follow the line of the brook to its source (only for the intrepid) or go up to Mill Hill and take The Ridgeway to the source.

For the latter alternative turn left at the line of trees and walk towards the ridge, rivulet on your right. Pass through an opening in the trees ahead and cross another playing field; a sports pavilion is ahead and slightly to the left. On reaching a stile (right) cross over it and again cross the next stile just over the lane. Now go diagonally across this large field passing the only tree in the field, an oak. Cross the next stile and follow the narrow path uphill.

This brings you out at The Ridgeway where the views south and north (the way we have just come) are tremendously impressive. The peculiar narrowness of the ridge is very apparent. (Bus 240.) Turn left for Mill Hill East underground station 3/4 mile (1.2km).

On reaching The Ridgeway turn right (west) and a walk of about 20 minutes will bring you to the splendid, winding and precipitous Holcombe Hill. At the foot of the hill is (left)

Lawrence Street where, directly opposite (right) is a stile into a large field which sweeps up to Totteridge. In this field the source of the Folly Brook stands unequivocally before us: a circle of trees and shrubs enclosing a pond, the brook gurgling forth. Appearing almost in the centre of a field, it is a textbook illustration of a source and startling in its simplicity. The ridges of Mill Hill and Totteridge and their joining Highwood Hill form the shapely basin which is drained by the little Folly.

For the return journey cross to the line of houses (Highwood Hill) for the 251 bus; this also goes to Edgware or Totteridge and Whetstone underground stations.

Alternatively, on reaching Highwood Hill turn left, go up the steep Holcombe Hill and in ½ mile (0.8km) you will reach the 240 bus for Mill Hill East underground station.

RIVER WANDLE

Introduction

The Wandle, prettiest of river names, was described early in the nineteenth century as the hardest worked river for its size in the world. In its 11 mile (17.5km) course it turned the wheels of no fewer than ninety watermills.

The reason for this powerful flow of water lay in the unusually steep incline of the river, a fact which made it useless for any form of navigation. The Wandle has two sources. The eastern source rises out of the chalk downs above Croydon and flows from the Waddon Ponds, while that to the west arises from vigorous springs at Carshalton. Both branches seem to come under almost immediate mutual attraction and their combined motive power coalesces at Hackbridge. The first 2 or 3 miles (3 or 4km), approximately the area around Mitcham, comprised the most vigorous section of the river and consequently the section most in demand.

Mills already existed on the Wandle in Saxon times for Domesday recorded thirteen. By 1600 there were 24, by 1700 68 and the climax of 90 mills was reached by the early nineteenth century. But the improvement in steam engines brought a disastrous decline, especially as water levels became erratic and began to fall. By 1850 only a third of the mills still operated. The decline then levelled out and during the last war there were three mills still able to supply emergency electricity: Ravensbury, Morden Hall and Liberty's Mill.

Regrettably the scenery north from Colliers Wood to Wandsworth has been shattered by industrial growth which prevents access to the river for long stretches. Although there

Waddon Ponds, the source of the Wandle

are short reaches which are attractive, and some industrial sections which are of interest to the specialist, the connecting route is mostly along main roads which are overloaded with traffic. Finally, the junction of the Wandle with the Thames is now a tip where rubbish is loaded onto barges.

As a result of the river's great commercial value many fine manor houses were built along the length of this ebullient, crystal clear river. Our walk will therefore reveal an abundance of industrial and social history as well as taking us through quite extraordinarily beautiful scenery.

14 Waddon Ponds to Colliers Wood
9 miles (14.5km)

Trains: Waddon (British Rail)
Buses: 130, 154, 157, 254, 289; London Country 403, 408;
    Green Line 725, 726, 777
Map: OS sheet no 176

Turn right out of the station and go to the traffic lights. Cross the road (Purley Way) and turn right. Shortly after continue straight across the Croydon Road. This brings you to Waddon Court Road.

Go up Waddon Court Road, pass Court Drive and the footpath bears round into a small park called Waddon Ponds. These were the manorial millponds belonging to Waddon Court but only this, the southern pond, remains. (Toilets to the right as you enter the park.) This little park is outstanding for its landscaping and general maintenance. The water, famed for its particular clarity, is well stocked with water plants, and there are plenty of moorhen and ducks to relish the pure water and its attendant rich growth.

On entering the park continue straight ahead going over a little bridge. Then bear right following along the bank of the pond. The path winds around with the exit just near the childrens' playground. On leaving the park turn right and come to Mill Lane, site of the cornmill which stood here until 1928. The estate of Waddon Court was then sold and developed for housing; fortunately the park was retained. Just across Mill Lane can be seen modern factory buildings. They have been built over the northern part of Waddon Ponds which was filled in in 1964.

Just before turning left into the Bridle Path there is a sluice over which water is pouring from the southern pond. The quantity is quite remarkable – 1.6 million gallons a day. This impressive waterpower, together with the western branch from Carshalton, was the reason for the great commercial success of the Wandle.

Now turn left into the Bridle Path. It runs parallel to a canalised section of the Wandle with small, attractive bun-

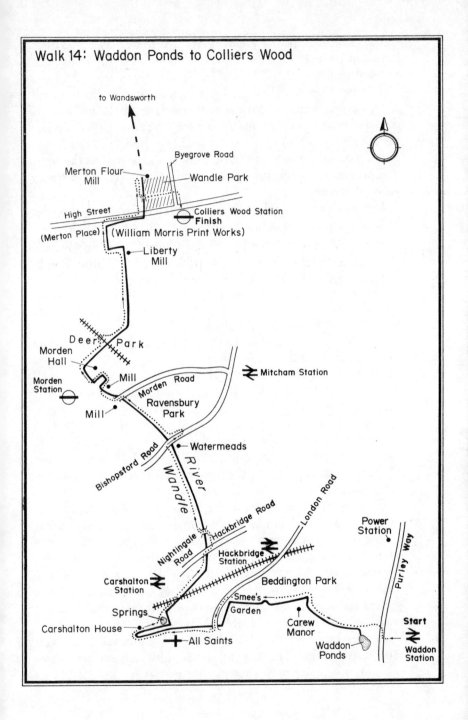

Walk 14: Waddon Ponds to Colliers Wood

galows on the opposite bank; there used to be watercress beds here until the 1930s. The path continues through a street of houses, still called the Bridle Path, and bears around to the right where we meet Bridges Lane. On the right is the fine, tall Victorian Beddington Mill, a mill site dating back to Domesday. It began as a corn mill but for the past two centuries it has been known as Lambert's snuff mill. To the left is The Brandries, a mellow range of old buildings, and across to the right can be seen a delightful small row of weatherboard cottages along the Wandle.

Make your way to the left of this small terrace and cross the little footbridge and continue along the right bank. All this part of the river is under very strict maintenance, canalised with edges shored up with wooden planks. At a junction of little streams turn right and continue along the right bank.

Continue to follow the river as it turns sharply to the right, but when it turns left shortly afterwards, having passed a weir, the path continues straight ahead. Over to the right you can look across to the cooling towers, white and shapely, of the power station on the Purley Way.

The path goes through an archway in the magnificent, high brick wall of Beddington Park; turn immediately left (Mallinson Road) following the wall. The path turns right into Crispin Crescent. Just where Crispin Crescent turns right again there is a small path to the left where we join up with the Wandle once more. Here we have reached Beddington Park with Carew Manor. Cross the river by the first small bridge and go towards the manor.

Archaeological evidence has revealed Stone Age settlements in this area; also Roman burial remains in coffins and urns. Domesday recorded two manors at Beddington which were later combined, about 1381, by Nicholas Carew into the present Carew Manor. The family lived here for five hundred years and it was not until 1859 when they finally departed that the manor was then rebuilt as an orphanage and the tradition was broken. It is now Carew Manor School, an attractive Victorian building that has the great Tudor hall preserved within its interior. There are large wrought-iron entrance gates with, opposite, a fine avenue of chestnut trees.

The church of St Mary the Virgin, Beddington

To the right of the manor is the church of St Mary the Virgin Beddington. Its origins date back to Saxon times but the present building dates from the fourteenth century. The attractive tower, crenellated, with strong angle buttresses and a northeast stair turret, was rebuilt in the earlier nineteenth century. The church contains many memorials to the Carew family and has the family chapel. There are two splendid lych gates in front of the church, the nearer one bearing the date of restoration, 1983. The idea of a lych gate, which has a small covering roof, was as a resting place for a coffin, 'lych' being Saxon for corpse.

On returning to the river you pass a delightful nineteenth-century cottage, a real 'Tudor' fantasy, and an impressive octagonal dovecote. It dates from the early eighteenth century but with its plain, soaring, vertical lines it could be modern. Beddington Park alone offers a good day out: café, childrens' playground, boating lake, putting green, tennis, cricket, football, carpark, fine architecture and, of course, the Wandle.

Back at the river cross the bridge and turn left. You soon come to a brick bridge wth stone facings, a charming mixture of Classical with Gothic detail: small classical columns with Corinthian capitals (many have been knocked off) and little Gothic arches with rosettes in the spandrels. It is very pretty with romantic steps curving down to the water. The water is crystal clear.

The path leads away from the water but it is preferable to keep to the bank walking over the grassy lawns. We pass several weirs on the way which remind us that the Wandle was noted for its vigour and capacity to drive watermills. We come to a flint and stone bridge which was the main crossing taking the private route from the London Road. The boating lake and bird sanctuary used to be the millpond of Wallington Manor.

To the right is a famous and beautiful decorative garden (open to the public) with many topiary trees and weeping willows. It was laid out by Arthur Smee (1818–77), who was an extraordinary man. He was surgeon to the Bank of England and distinguished himself by his remarkably inventive approach to surgical techniques which included the use of electricity for theraputic purposes. Later in life he became interested in horticulture and not only produced this beautiful garden but published the research which he made in a learned study in 1872 (*My Garden, its Plan and Culture*), which was illustrated with over a thousand wood engravings.

Keep to the path, which has swung back to our route, and it will bring you to the London Road (buses 127 and 234 with Hackbridge railway station within walking distance to the right). On leaving the park, cross straight over the London Road to the fine Bridge House (1770) (three storeys with central portico) and turn left.

This is a busy road but nevertheless attractive with water channels and springs running along both sides. At the Rose and Crown (which serves food) the road curves round to the left (Manor Road North). At the traffic lights turn right into Acre Lane (opposite Duke's Head) and once past the Fox and Hounds we enter Carshalton. There is a delightful village atmosphere, and not surprisingly this is an area designated as of outstanding interest.

The powerful springs, which are the western source of the Wandle, have long been famed for their waters. Its Saxon name, Aewiell-tun, by the well or spring, records its early significance. The later prefix 'Cars-' may refer to cress, watercress, which grew successfully in the pure water. All

Saints Church (left), although subject to much rebuilding, contains some early work including the Lady Chapel of about 1200.

Continuing ahead into Pound Street, there is another and larger pond to the right and nearby the fine Carshalton House. It dates from the late seventeenth century but had a number of alterations carried out during the eighteenth century, notably the 'Blue Room' in Adam style sometime after the 1760s. In the garden there is a remarkable waterhouse and an elaborate grotto known as The Hermitage. The house has been a school for nearly a hundred and fifty years and is now St Philomena's Convent; it may be viewed by application to the Sister Superior. Of its distinguished residents, Dr John Radcliffe was the benefactor responsible for the Radcliffe Library (1749) in Oxford. He was Royal Physician to Queen Anne whom he offended by not attending her in her final illness on the grounds that he was himself indisposed. He died at Carshalton House in 1714 only three months after the queen.

Return to the first pond (opposite the church) and walk along it with the water to your left. We will now trace the western source of the Wandle with a branch flowing north to reach the eastern branch (which we have already walked) at Hackbridge.

The path leads into a delightful small park known as The Grove, and we follow the stream keeping it on the left. Grove House (1825) stands within the park. Crossing a small bridge, we leave the path and enter Mill Lane and turn right. The river is running parallel to Mill Lane but is hidden behind the line of buildings (right). At Butter Hill there are copious beds of watercress, with a raw peppery flavour, again growing in crystal clear water. After going under the railway bridge look for Strawberry Lodge (left) which dates from about 1700.

Continue along River Gardens where the path moves back to the bank still on the left of the river. At a waterfall the lane bears left to a small loop that curves round to join the eastern branch of the Wandle where it flows in from the right. This whole area was of great industrial importance with large numbers of watermills involved in a wide variety of trades – copper, gunpowder, oil, fulling, wool, leather and snuff – all now departed. The river bed is a healthy gravel and not the usual river mud.

At Nightingale Road where we turn right, go over the bridge (Hack Bridge) and cross the road to rejoin the river on its right bank. Go over the white bridge which can be seen ahead, and we come to an island which is at the centre of the divided river. At Culvers Avenue (bus 293) turn left and we can see the line of trees which follows the course of the river. Cross Culvers Avenue to those trees and continue with the water to your right. There is a large modern housing estate on the left and small inter-war houses to the right. The river here is very narrow and rich in plant life, especially bamboo. There is also a lovely growth of poplars all the way along the course of the river. This is, in fact, a small branch of the Wandle, the main course of which, three times the width of this little section, soon flows in from the right. The path, just bare earth, goes through pleasantly natural scenery, no landscaping here, and we pass behind Wandle Valley Hospital.

Cross over Middleton Road and straight ahead is Watermead Lane. The outfall from Beddington Sewage Farm enters the river and straight away the water drops from grade A2 to grade D; a regrettable use of the river but one which might be discontinued. Further downstream the water is purified again and pumped back to Carshalton through pipes which are laid along the river bed itself.

Bishopsford House, in a prominent position on raised ground over to the left, has traces of the old track of the Surrey Iron Railway, the oldest railway in the world. It was opened in 1803 and ran from Wandsworth to Croydon and later to Carshalton and to Merstham. Its special purpose was to serve the extensive milling industry which lined the banks of the Wandle. It was really a horse-drawn tram running on rails but it contained the idea of what was later to develop into the railway proper. Similar horse-drawn railways had been used before for hauling goods within industrial sites, but these were for private use. The greatly reduced friction of wheels running on rails meant that one horse could pull a load of over 30 tons. This accounted for its successful span of over forty years before the steam railway superseded it in 1846.

The path moves slightly to the left away from the river, but keep to the path: going nearer to the water brings you into dense growth. The scenery is particularly luxurious and of a rather limpid quality. To the right is the National Trust property of Watermeads, a nature park which lies behind a high, wire fence. Twelve acres of land known as the Watermeads were given to the Trust in 1913 to maintain a wildlife sanctuary. The Trust merely keeps open the path around the area but otherwise allows it to follow the course of nature. Consequently the natural habitat and freedom from intrusion had produced an area rich in birdlife, including herons and kingfishers. As you approach Bishopsford Road you will see three weatherboard cottages (right) built in 1760 as fishermen's cottages, illustrating the rich supply of trout which came from the Wandle. Arrangements for obtaining access to Watermeads may be discussed with the National Trust (42 Queen Anne's Gate, London SW1).

On reaching Bishopsford Road (there is a beautiful view of Watermeads and the fishermen's cottages), cross straight over and turn right following along a high wall (bus 280, Mitcham railway station is a short walk to the right). At the end of the wall turn sharp left and double-back along the other side of the wall to rejoin the Wandle. Here, on an island site, stood Mitcham Grove, one-time home of Clive of India. It was demolished in 1860. More recently this area was a cricket field before development as a council housing estate.

We enter Ravensbury Park, a nice example of a carefully planned area of lawns, trees, flowerbeds and water. It is a delightful public amenity and has been a park since 1930 when the old Ravensbury Manor was demolished. Continue over an iron bridge, and at the next iron bridge cross over and turn left bringing you down to the boating lake. Follow the lake with the water to your left. Do not cross the next bridge but continue ahead (a detour to the right leads to toilets) where we go along an avenue of enormous plane trees. Cross the next bridge which goes over the river and a little canal with an energetic weir.

This brings you to Morden Road which you should cross straight over and turn left. From here you can now see the old

131

Ravensbury Mill, the first of two superb mills that we shall see in this area. It was a famous snuff mill with a tradition extending back to the mid-eighteenth century. During the last war an experiment was tried to use it as an emergency electricity generator but the fine mill wheels, still existing inside the building, were not suited to the nature of the task. For some years it was used by a manufacturer of sports goods but now its handsome exterior has its ground floor windows bricked up. Continue along Morden Hall Road, the wall to your right, until you reach the large gates of Morden Cottage which you enter. On the left is part of the old moat which surrounded Morden Hall. Also on the left are the marvellous old stables with a clocktower surmounting an archway.

Morden Hall and Park occupies the site of very ancient settlements. The old Roman road of Stane Street (London to Chichester) runs across the park just a few feet below the surface. An Anglo-Saxon document reveals that Morden belonged to Westminster Abbey and this is confirmed in the Domesday Book.

At the Dissolution of the Monasteries (1535–40) Richard Garth became lord of the manor and it remained in the family for over three hundred years. The only other owners were the Hatfields (1872–1941) before it came to the National Trust. Now the London Borough of Merton has its offices here. They include the delightful registry office which is housed in the former snuff mill; wedding parties can stroll on the lawns beside the Wandle. The mill had already been established in the eighteenth century by the Hatfields before they bought the Hall. It closed down in 1922 but fortunately one of its two millwheels, very narrow but of large diameter, is still in place. It too was used for emergency electricity during the last war.

Retrace your steps past the stables, converted now for use by National Trust officers. Do not go through the arch but keep close to the stable wall and continue ahead to a small iron gate which returns you to the moat (should the gate be closed return to the main road, turn right and continue to Merton Library where you can pick up the route – see below). Having gone through the gate you then cross an attractive iron bridge and walk directly towards Morden Hall passing along the left side.

The present Hall dates from about 1700 but was considerably altered around 1840, the evident work making this rather a hybrid building but not without the usual charms associated with the type. The setting comes to the rescue. The surrounding Park and Deer Park retain a spacious, leisurely dignity imparted by the broad meadows, the lines of trees and the picturesque courses of the Wandle and its various cuttings.

On leaving the grounds and emerging onto the main road, there is a wide choice of buses (80 and 93 in the immediate vicinity) and Morden underground station, the southern terminus of the Northern line, which is straight ahead on London Road.

To continue the walk, however, turn right on leaving Morden Hall. When you draw level with Merton Library (left across the road) take the little wooden gate in the wall beside you. This takes you into the Deer Park. There is no path but a worn track follows the stream, which is on your right. When you reach the overhead powerlines and a small bridge (which you do not cross), turn left towards distant buildings. You reach a fence; follow along until you come to a gate, which you pass through, and then go over the footbridge which crosses the Wimbledon to Croydon railway line. It was constructed in 1855 thereby cutting off the old road which went through the park.

The path now follows the river again. You cross Windsor Avenue and continue ahead along a very pleasant route. This is parallel to powerlines but where they turn right you will hear the rushing of water. Get down close to the river and here you will see a fine waterwheel. It is known as Liberty's Print Works, alas now closed.

The mill was started in 1724 by William Halshide as a calico printers. It continued to produce block printing when it was taken over early in the nineteenth century by Edmund Littler. Liberty's began placing some of their fabric printing work with Littler's firm until later in the nineteenth century they were undertaking practically all of Liberty's work. By the turn of the century this famous shop had immense influence, not only over fashion but also in the world of art. It was a natural step, therefore, for Liberty's to take over these works in 1904 and keep the waterwheel turning for themselves. This wheel was constructed in 1885 and has huge, wide blades and looks as powerful and as durable as it proved to be when, during the last war, it was used to produce electricity. This is one of the best preserved sites of industrial archaeology in the country. The last hand-printing for Liberty's was done by a husband and wife team in the early 1970s. Up to twenty-four hand-cut wooden blocks might be used on a typical 'Indian' design so only some 30yd (27m) could be produced daily. When this team retired this beautiful, but costly, process came to an end. Now the printing is done by machine using the silk-screen process.

All the land from here north to Merton High Street was owned by the Augustinian Merton Priory (1114–1538) which was demolished at the Dissolution. The important Statute of Merton (1235) is the earliest in the statute book and resulted from a decision taken at Merton Priory. Both Thomas à Becket and Walter de Merton were educated at the Priory. Walter, a Chancellor of England, was founder of Merton College Oxford (see Walk 10).

Now enter Station Road which is on line with the Roman Stane Street. There is no through route straight ahead but the large paper mills which can be seen on the right bank of the river was the site of William Morris' printing works (1881–1940); this tradition dated back to 1752 and to a Domesday corn mill before that. At Station Road turn left and then first right along Abbey Road.

Abbey Road marks the eastern boundary of Merton Place (built 1699) where Nelson lived. It was bought for him by Lady Hamilton. They lived with Lady Hamilton's husband, Sir William Hamilton, in a *ménage à trois* from 1801, the year of the birth of her daughter, Horatia, by Nelson, until Nelson's death in 1805 when the house was sold. It was demolished in 1823. Both Nelson and Lady Hamilton used to fish in the Wandle, and she had a channel made from the river to bring its clear waters to Merton Place. Ornamental streams and ponds were made which she called 'The Nile' to commemorate his famous battle of 1798. Nelson's association with Merton is recalled in a number of local placenames.

Continue to the T-junction with Merton High Street, passing the Princess Royal en route. Turn right at the High Street and keep to the right for an urban view of the Wandle. The water, flowing out from underneath a factory, is about 30ft (9m) broad. At the road junction cross over left and go along Wandle Bank. The attractive Wandle Terrace (1864) was rebuilt too severely in 1977 with unsuitable tip-up windows and stainless steel vents. Bank Buildings, a row of five little houses, shows what restoration really should be like, and Devonshire Cottages is another attractive pair.

This straight section of water along Wandle Bank is a short canal which was made to serve the old Merton Flour Mill which is ahead at the top of the street. Originating in the eighteenth century, this fine building, the water flowing under an imposing arch, is now used by the firm of leather-dressers, Connolly Brothers. The mill used to be owned by a friend of Nelson's, James Perry, who lived at Wandle Bank House from 1790 to 1821. Retrace your steps to the entrance into the park which was the grounds of Perry's house, now owned by the National Trust. Continue ahead across the park where there are fountain relics of the old house and a short section of the original River Wandle.

The northern continuation of the river has been extensively altered and runs through arid wastes of industrial land so it is appropriate to complete the walk at this point. Although King George's Park in Southfields contains an attractive stretch of the river the unpleasant means of reaching it by lengthy main roads fairly spoils the memories of the upper river. Railway enthusiasts, however, can turn left at Byegrove Road (straight ahead) and continue to Mead Path. This is a narrow lane occupying part of the former track of the old Surrey Iron Railway.

To complete the walk, turn right (south) on reaching Byegrove Road and right again at Colliers Wood High Street. Colliers Wood underground station is just over on the left. Buses 57, 88, 131, 155, and 200.

DARTFORD CREEK

Introduction

Kent has always been in the forefront of our relationship with the Continent. In fact, it used to have a physical connection with the European landmass. When, some seven to ten thousand years ago, the network of rivers overflowed into one vast waterway, as the south-east corner of England tipped down into the sea, the English Channel was formed. With only 21 miles (34km) separating Kent from the Continent it became the natural landing place for traders and invaders.

The River Darent, known in its lower reaches as the Dartford Creek, has a place in the history of the south-east and continually features in the changing uses of the area. It rises in the Kentish Weald near Westerham and flows east before running north through Otford, Eynsford and Dartford, where it is joined by the River Cray flowing in from the west, and enters the Thames opposite Purfleet. Both the Darent and Cray were the sites of Stone Age settlements and many flint artefacts have been found in evidence. Europe's oldest fossil skull was found not far away at Swanscombe, and bones of bear, bison, elephant, lion and rhinoceros have been discovered along the animal and river courses of prehistoric times. Celtic tribes inhabited the banks of these rivers, and Celtic origins can be traced in the names of rivers of the south-east: Darent, Cray, Stour and Medway. In fact, Kent itself is a name of Celtic origin.

When the Romans began their conquest of England under Aulus Plautius in AD43 (Caesar having made exploratory forays in 55 and 54BC), their route from Deal to London (a route later called Watling Street) took them across three rivers, the Medway, Darent and Cray. Roman towns eventually sprang up at the crossing places: Rochester, Dartford and Crayford, respectively. With characteristic efficiency, the Romans settled themselves in comfort, and villas have been excavated at Dartford and along the Darent valley. All the evidence is that the Darent was part of an important Roman settlement with well-developed transportation routes both by road and river.

Long before the Romans left England in about AD410 the south-east had been raided by fierce tribes from the Baltic coast of North Germany; raids which caused the Romans to build forts along the Kentish coast. When the Romans finally withdrew, tribes of Angles, Saxons and Jutes surged in. The Jutes in particular settled in Kent where they formed a close-knit community. Their units of government, known as 'Lathes', remained unique to this county and the Domesday Book in 1086 gave details of those laws which were peculiar to Kent. Jutish settlements, burial sites and many artefacts, including much beautiful jewellery, have been unearthed all along the Darent river.

A period of three hundred years elapsed before the onslaught of the Danish invasions upset the by-now routine agricultural tradition of the Anglo-Saxon nation. What attracted the Danes to Kent, for here they brought large armies rather than their customary hit-and-run raiding parties, was the presence of great monasteries such as that at Canterbury. In Kent King Alfred scored major victories against the Danes at Rochester and Milton Regis and even succeeded in baptising the two sons of the Dane, Haeston.

The Domesday Book devotes twenty-eight pages to Kent. William the Conqueror was determined that this part of the vulnerable south-east should be in the hands of his most trusted subjects. Accordingly, his half-brother Odo, Bishop of Bayeux, was made Earl of Kent and received almost two hundred manors of which six were along the River Darent and five were along the River Cray. In the twelfth century, pilgrimages to the shrine of Thomas à Becket, murdered in Canterbury Cathedral in 1170, began a vast tourist industry that had economic significance all along the road to Canterbury for some three hundred years. Chaucer's pilgrims in the *Canterbury Tales,* written in the 1380s, crossed the River Darent at Dartford, its Dominican and Franciscan monasteries forming part of the busy chain of halfway houses.

It was during the Tudor period that the River Darent began five hundred years of industrial tradition. Henry strengthened the south-east of England as a front-line of defence and therefore transportation by barge along the Darent was of vital importance for its iron, gunpowder and ship-building industries. When the Spanish Armada approached in 1588, Kent was ready and nearly fifty pitch-burning beacons, placed within a system of sight-lines, flared up the warning.

The prosperity of Elizabethan England also came to the River Darent. Its ample depth of water and good position in relation to London and down the Thames Estuary to provincial or foreign towns made it an industrial asset. The second paper mill in England was sited early in Elizabeth's reign on the river at Dartford; large quantities of water are required in this industry. The success of this mill can be gauged from the fact that it quickly expanded to employ six hundred men, an enormous workforce for that time.

In the days before properly engineered roads, navigable waterways played an important role in passenger transport. A popular route from London to Kent was along the Thames and then along the River Darent to Dartford and all the way up to Otford, a journey which was still made until the early nineteenth century.

Developments of major importance to the Darent and Cray rivers occurred in 1840 when commissioners were appointed to undertake improvements which included the straightening of certain sections by making artificial cuts. The scheme arose from mutual discussion between local landowners and traders with the aim of bringing general benefit to the area. It was to be non-profit-making; even the commissioners were unpaid. But so great was its success that profits, in fact, did accrue, so that tolls were actually reduced. Commissioners for the Dartford and Crayford Navigations still control the area and are still unpaid.

And so the pattern continued down to the twentieth century. Engineering, explosives, chemicals, paper, cloth, silk, linen-thread, flour mills and market-gardening trades were supplying national and international markets from the wharfs of the River Darent and its companion the River Cray. Although this activity is now greatly reduced, the really historical section of the Darent from Dartford to the Thames is still redolent of its former industrial strength while the lower reaches possess the typically open landscape and exhilarating spaciousness of the Thames Estuary.

15 Dartford to the Thames
7 miles (11km) (circular walk)

Trains: Dartford (British Rail)
Buses: 96; London Country 402, 477, 480, 492, 494;
      Green Line 725, 726, 755
Map: OS sheet no 177

On leaving Dartford station turn right immediately you reach
the road (Home Gardens). At the corner with Hythe Street
turn right and go under the railway bridge. Continue straight
ahead, across the junction with Mill Pond Road, to the continuation of Hythe Street. Here, on the right, is Dartford
Wharfage Company, an old firm and still the largest users of
the Dartford Creek. Next is The Pheonix pub and, nearby,
three old cottages and a plaque stating 'Nelson Row 1806', all
that remains of the old area that used to surround the town
wharf. Take the narrow lane beside the pub and about 80yd
(72m) further along you come to the imposing town basin.

From the footbridge which crosses the water you can see, to
the south, the course of the river (left) and (right) a large dock
curving out of view behind factories and warehouses. Looking
north, a long straight reach leads to the lock. Take the path
running along the right bank of Dartford creek. Commercial
premises line both sides of the creek so it is good to see that this
path has been kept open.

The lock, opened in 1895, is of very considerable size with
the lock-keeper's cottage alongside. It was built by the commissioners who were also responsible for the lock-keeper's
cottage, an office and the bascule bridge which we have already
crossed. The lock is a magnificent one with a lock basin beside
it and a controllable weir. The path now takes us up to the top
of the flood wall. This gives us a splendid view of the Wiggins
Teape paper factory which is continuing a long-established industry on the Dartford Creek.

The factory was built in 1862 and was occupied by a number
of different firms before Wiggins Teape. The factory began
with two paper mills and this number increased to a maximum
of eight mills in 1958. Since then they have decreased to the

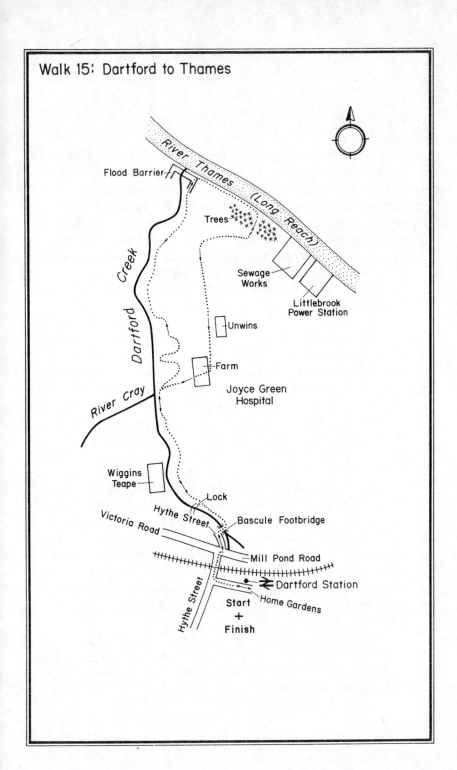

Walk 15: Dartford to Thames

present single large mill which is capable of turning out 7 tons of paper an hour. Until the late 1970s, wood pulp was brought from Scandinavia by large cargo boats which moored in the Thames and loaded the pulp on to barges for the remainder of the journey up the Dartford Creek. Now the deliveries are made by road but fuel oil is still brought in by barge.

Over to the right lie expansive meadows with allotments and herds of cows. You will see how low down the meadows are from our vantage point on top of the flood wall. In the distance are the twin chimneys of Littlebrook Power Station. It is a splendid view, spacious and full of contrast. The creek has a very considerable tidal rise and fall. At low tide the water recedes to a mere trickle along a central channel. At high tide it has a satisfying fullness of water – almost voluptuous – between the creek's firmly delineated banks. We then come to a familiar river site: a breaker's yard with cars piled high on the land and boats sadly awaiting their turn at their last moorings.

Now the factories are left behind. The land opens out on both sides and the path takes two huge loops as it skirts deep, reed-filled bays which are flooded at high tide. These bays mark the former route of the creek before it was straightened by the Navigation. At the end of the second loop the River Cray (about the same width as the Dartford Creek) flows in from the west; it rises at the Priory Gardens in Orpington. Barges still use the River Cray for deliveries of grain to Allied Mills and oil to Century Oils and Dussek Campbell Oils.

On either side of the creek we have marshes: Crayford to the left and Dartford Salt Marshes on our side. Their 'dry' appearance is evidence of the efficiency of the high bank that we are walking along. Looking ahead you will see the vital link in these flood defences: the flood barrier at the mouth of the creek where it flows into the Thames. Although a map of the area suggests that the marshes are featureless, they are, in fact, a warren of pathways and hedgerows dividing up the fields. Continue on to the flood barrier.

The flood barrier began service in November 1982 after a period of trials which lasted for just over a year. The design consists of two drop-leaf gates between two tall towers, one on either side of the water. Planning went parallel with that of the main flood barrier at Woolwich for it was possible that when closing the Woolwich barrier a surge-tide could rebound into the creeks downstream – hence the flood barriers at Dartford, Crayford and Barking.

The Dartford barrier is visited each morning and afternoon every day of the year. Inspections are carried out and other water installations and sluices are also inspected. When high tides are anticipated the barrier is manned for a twelve-hour period before high water. During its first year of operation there were four or five emergency calls and then the gates were closed as a safeguard. The barrier is controlled by Southern Water Authority which is also responsible for the drainage and clear passage of the Darent and Cray rivers. However, Thames Water Authority is responsible for checking pollution and fisheries so the authorities work together on the same areas of water. Before the flood barrier was built, in 1977–78, very high tides caused flooding which forced some people to leave their homes and businesses in Dartford and others to sand-bag their front doors.

Go past the barrier and continue on to the River Thames and follow the path downstream with the Thames on your left. It is a rugged but interesting walk with the varied shapes of the industrial buildings over on the Purfleet side. Notice how high we are walking up upon the flood wall. Keep a look-out for the tree-filled area which comes up on your right for we have to take a path through its centre.

We are now on Long Reach, a straight stretch of water that contains a measured mile that was used for speed trials of ships. It is the longest reach upstream from Tilbury. The name Long Reach used to strike a chill note for it was here, in 1903, that the Metropolitan Asylums Board built an isolation hospital for persons from London who were suffering from infectious diseases, notably smallpox. Sufferers were brought from London by river then loaded by crane onto a horse-drawn tram and brought to the Joyce Green Hospital. In the 1920s it was used mainly when there was an epidemic, and during the last war it became a conventional hospital, being absorbed into the National Health Service in 1948. The old isolation buildings were sited near the Thames; they were deliberately destroyed by fire in 1977 to make sure that no infection remained. The site was then taken over by the adjoining Thames Water Authority works. The hospital's name is derived from Joyce Green Farm which used to occupy the site. First mentioned in documents dating from 1690, there is no conclusive evidence that the name referred either to a place or to a person. Today the hospital has six hundred beds and has taken over much of the work of Dartford's general hospital which closed down in the 1960s.

While still high up on our vantage point on the flood wall we can see the sewage works ahead of us and, beyond that, the tall chimneys of Littlebrook Power Station. Long Reach Treatment and Sewage Works opened in 1877 and was under the West Kent Authority before being taken over by the Thames Water Authority in 1974. It serves an area which includes Dartford and Crayford and extends to Sevenoaks. The drainage system runs parallel to the River Darent. The treatment process takes place almost entirely in the open air and the grounds have been attractively landscaped.

Littlebrook Power Station comes under the South Eastern Region of the Central Electricity Generating Board. The com-

Littlebrook Power Station on the Thames

plete station first went into operation in January 1983 and, as might be expected, it is one of the most up to date in terms of technology and equipment. It uses oil-fired boilers and the fuel is delivered to the station by some of the largest vessels to be seen on the Thames. For the convenience of these deliveries and for the supply of vast quantities of water which are required in the generating process, the station is sited as closely as possible to the river. To the layman, however, the station's principal virtue is its sheer good looks. Smooth walls, differently coloured blocks, elegant white chimneys and an overall compact form make this a really attractive industrial design.

Our route continues to the middle of the small forest of trees (right) where you will see a narrow road, a track almost, running at right angles away from the shore and going due south. You will have to scramble down the steep bank of the flood wall. Beneath the dusty track are the remains of an old cobbled road. In about 50yd (45m) it divides, but keep to the track which bears slightly to the right. A distinct right bend further on brings you out of the trees and onto a fairly straight path. All around are salt marshes. The growth is very green and little patches of water can be seen glistening beneath the long grass. Everywhere a network of little canals drains away the surplus water.

At the T-junction we come to yet another rugged dirt road. Turn left; going right would take you back to the flood barrier. The road becomes made up and we pass (left) Unwin's Pyrotechnics Factory which reminds us of the large explosives industry which existed in this area until after the last war. The little tin shacks of this factory conform to the tradition of manufacturing explosives in small buildings to minimise the damage in the event of an accidental blast.

Further on you will see several old notices warning of explosives and fines of £5 for unauthorised entry to what are now open fields for all the factories have gone. The notices refer to the Explosives Act of 1875. At one time the traffic along this little country road would have been intense; and along the Dartford Creek too where the materials and munitions would have been handled by water-borne transport. After the disastrous floods of 1953, when there was serious loss of life at

Canvey Island further down the Thames, the explosives industry here, also affected by those floods, took the decision not to store materials in this area for the whole of the low-lying land was flooded to a depth of 8ft (2.4m). Vickers had the main explosives factory and finally left about 1960. A related industry was Ferranti's missile-producing units and they were the last to leave. However, the area is still licensed for the manufacture of explosives.

You come to a farm (right) where the last building is a fairly new bungalow with a steep red roof. Permission may be sought to take the path past the bungalow but do remember to close the gates. The farm owner was here during the 1953 flooding and lost a lot of livestock and equipment. The path over the fields brings you back to the creek quite near to the breaker's yard which we passed on the earlier part of our walk. During out walk the tide will have changed so the creek may now have a very different appearance. On reaching the water, turn left with the creek on your right. Retrace the route which you took earlier: pass the lock and go along the narrow path that runs between the backs of factories and the creek.

On reaching the bridge go over it and along the lane back to The Pheonix. Turn left into Hythe Street, continuing straight ahead and under the railway bridge. Then, immediately left is Home Gardens with the station entrance further along on your left.

THE SAXON SHORE WAY

Introduction

This invigorating route is perhaps more of a hike than a walk. Stout shoes, even boots, and at times good weather-proof clothing are required. And perhaps some sustenance too for once you leave the Ship and Lobster at Denton Wharf, just outside Gravesend, you are well and truly on your own.

Our walk takes in part of the Gravesend and Lower Hope reaches. It passes from the flurry of cranes, wharfs and shipping of Tilbury Docks (across on the north shore) and Gravesend's remnants of gentility, to the superb watery views of the water-filled quarries at Cliffe. Here, as the Thames turns sharply north from Coalhouse Point, the river seems infinitely wide as we gaze northwards to the shimmering white oil tanks of Thameshaven. In fact, we are gazing along, not across, the river, but the illusion creates an enormous feeling of spaciousness, especially if the sun is setting.

The sea walls which are to be found in many parts of the Thames Estuary have their origins as far back as the Romans in the fourth century AD, but it was in the thirteenth century that the present 140 miles (224km) of wall from Gravesend to Rye were established. Also during that century a violent land disturbance set back the shore line so that in places the old wall is now 7 miles (11.2km) inland. The land on both shores is very low-lying, even below sea level in many places, and has continued to fall at the rate of about 1ft (0.3m) each century.

147

16 Gravesend to Cliffe
6 or 12 miles (9.5 or 19km)

Trains: Gravesend (British Rail)
Bus Enquiries: London Country Bus Service: Gravesend
             66267; Green Line: 74, 424, 11 (Reigate)
Map: OS sheet no 178

On reaching Gravesend make for the clocktower, a tall Gothic structure situated at the centre of a crossroads. Take Milton Road into Ordnance Road and left into Canal Road which brings you onto the river front. Here can be seen the basin of what was the Thames and Medway Canal. Although we shall see a stretch of the canal further on, the project was a failure and has now been almost completely filled in. It was begun in 1801. The 7 miles (11.2km) to Rochester took over twenty years to construct for the line of the canal had to pass through terrain of the densest mud and clay and required the construction of a 2½ mile (4km) tunnel through hills of the Hundred of Hoo. The decision to build seemed a good one: it would greatly reduce the long journey round the Isle of Grain to Rochester and the Naval Dockyards at Chatham. Also, as it was during the Napoleonic Wars, it would avoid contact with enemy ships which were engaged in hit-and-run activities in the Estuary. However, the canal was not completed until long after Napoleon's defeat. Commercial users were then not greatly interested: long waits to catch the tides to enter the basin often made it as quick, and certainly cheaper, to go the long way round. The railway line was then built to run along beside the canal (it still does) and also, extraordinarily, to share the tunnel with the canal; quite a squeeze until the canal was filled in. However, the basin together with its lock is now maintained as the headquarters of the Gravesend Yacht Club which was founded in 1894.

The view here across the Thames is notably spacious for it is about three times the width which we have been used to in town. Looking across to the left there is a lattice-work of cranes at Tilbury Docks and possibly a large Russian liner drawn up at the landing-stage which gives deep-water mooring.

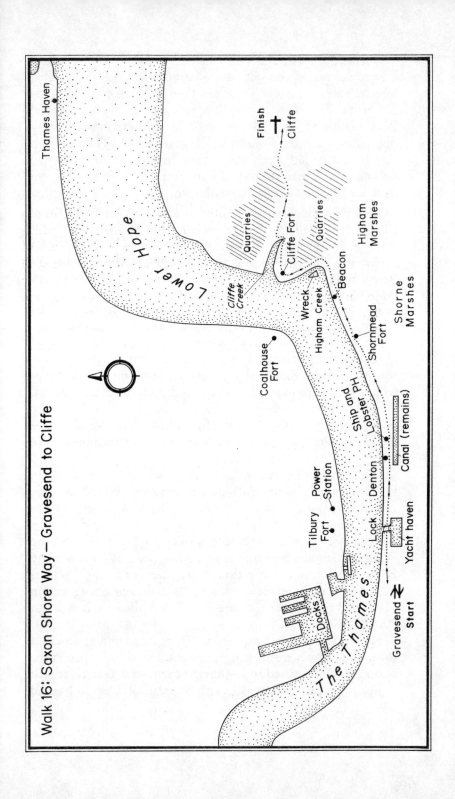

Walk 16: Saxon Shore Way – Gravesend to Cliffe

During the 1960s and 1970s the Port of London suffered decreasing use as more and more container ships were being used which required deeper moorings than London could supply. However, deep moorings were possible at Tilbury. Gravesend Reach is broad, straight and .deep so Tilbury offered every opportunity for development. The scope of the Thames from now on can be judged by the fact that in under 10 miles (16km) downstream super tankers of a quarter of a million tons and over are able to dock at Thameshaven.

Directly opposite, on the north bank, are the enormous chimneys of Tilbury Power Station which, throughout our walk, will remain a landmark. Further to the right the landmass drops to a mere pencil line, the low-lying land which the sea wall must protect. Between docks and power station can be seen the low, round towers of Tilbury Fort.

The fort began as a small defence initiated by Henry VIII which, in time, became an encampment of major importance. Together with the fort at Gravesend, no invader was prepared to test their crossfire. The most famous event in Tilbury's history was Queen Elizabeth I's visit in 1588 to the 17,000 troops which were stationed there awaiting the advent of the Spanish Armada. Elizabeth delivered her famous speech to boost the morale of the troops. It is the first of four very similar forts which we shall see on our walk emphasising the importance attached to defence in this area.

Continue along the front, cross the lock and carry on along the lane which winds through timberyards. Where the lane turns sharply right and then left, all the timberyards on the right have been built on the filled-in space of the old Thames and Medway Canal. The lane now runs into the small made-up Wharf Road which brings us to a crossroads. We will shortly be turning left in the direction of the cranes of Denton Wharf, but briefly continue ahead a few yards to the remaining section of the old canal which, at present, is not filled in. It is about 200yd (180m) long.

Now make that left turn from Wharf Road and go towards the cranes which are sticking up beyond roof-tops. Just at the corner of Wharf Road and where we turn left is a concrete post indicating a public footpath with the sign of a Saxon horned helmet: a good and appropriate sign. We will see it again as the wall is further extended. The road broadens to a fairly wide service area. Denton Wharf, with its busy cluster of cranes, handles the containers which can be seen stored in high stacks to the right. Continue straight ahead to the narrow way marked 'Private Road. Access to Ship and Lobster only.' This brings you to a plain, but welcome pub strangely isolated in a perimeter of wire fences and, on the river side, hard against the new concrete sea wall. A notice states 'Flood Defence Works 1982–1983'. If you go inside you will see that the pub is actually at first-floor level because of flooding in the past.

This latest wall will be the new line of defence against the sea. Massive mounds of earth have been bulldozed to great heights all along our route. There is quite a pleasant stretch of even-sized shingle at Denton Wharf. On a good day there are fishermen and others taking the sun. Denton Wharf is the last little community before we strike out onto the open shore.

Further along there are two narrow wooden piers running out into the river. The second carries an endless belt for off-loading sand and gravel from dredgers; graded mounds of different materials can be seen to the right. Apart from building use, the river also supplies some of the raw materials for cement manufacture and for the production of explosives.

This stretch of the river usually contains a number of vessels anchored before moving on to their moorings, and you may hear the occasional small-arms fire from the shooting range. One is reminded that the manufacture of explosives was one of the traditional industries of this area up to the last war. Although the north shore has signs of industry (you can just begin to see the white oil tanks of Thameshaven) our side is almost devoid of any activity.

Shorne Marshes lie to the right with the hills of Higham and Cliffe beyond and Shornmead Fort comes up directly on our track. The forts in this area are built to a pattern. Tilbury and Coalhouse forts on the north shore and Shornmead and Cliffe forts on the south have semicircular fronts to the river which enabled the gun-emplacements to be deployed up- and downstream as well as straight ahead. They were built very low indeed. Walls are understandably thick. The guns, no longer

Shornmead Fort

existing, were mounted in solid blocks of iron which were set within deep granite arches. The stone work is massive and well executed. At Shornmead there are eleven gun mountings which are still clearly visible. But the rear of the fort can no longer be made out for huge stone and concrete sections have been scattered away from their original positions.

Shornmead, together with the other forts, has never fired a shot at an invader. Although the Estuary looks invitingly wide invaders were well aware of the extremely twisting route of the Thames, especially nearer to London, and of the treacherous currents and sandbanks which were known only to skilled Thames watermen.

After Shornmead Fort keep well up on the new wall; going further to the shore will involve awkward and circuitous routes around the creeks and cuttings which lie ahead. Ahead too we can see the bright red-painted Shornmead Beacon. This beacon marks the southern bank where the river turns north almost at a right angle. As the river runs away to the north we can look along it lengthways and obtain a stupendous view of an uninterrupted 3 miles (4.8km) to the distant shore of Thameshaven. At full tide when the saltings, the shallow mud flats which quickly become exposed at low water, can be included in the river's expanse the dramatic inland sea of Lower Hope Reach is one of London's great sights. It is also the last of the river's reaches before Sea Reach runs out into the open sea.

Higham Creek is a sizeable bay which is easily recognised after passing Shornmead Beacon. It is man-made in fact. Much of the ragged shoreline was created by the 'muddies' of earlier times. These were men who came to these shores on the falling tides, letting their barges settle on the mud. They would fill a barge with many tons of mud which was used for building and manufacturing explosives, then float off with the rising tide. It was a killing job which had to be undertaken at all hours to suit the tides: by the light of oil lamps at night. The spade with which they dug the mud was of an ingenious design. Made of wood, it had a metal plate which was sprung along the cutting edge which would throw off the mud when flung into the barge. The incursions into the shoreline, however, caused considerable disfigurement. Higham Creek is just one of many shallow cuttings which drain or fill with the tides in matters of minutes. When you reach the landward extremity of the creek leave the wall and follow around the north-east shoreline of the creek.

At the far side you will make out an old wrecked hulk; you will find it marked on some maps. As you approach you will see the remains of the vast wooden hull of a sailing ship listing deeply into the mud. All superstructure is gone but the timbers that remain are impressive. Further on lies another fort, Cliffe Fort. The man most responsible for the reconstruction of the defences in this area was General Gordon of Khartoum fame. He undertook the work from 1865 to 1871. Behind the fort at Cliffe is a large rectangular barracks: austere granite, regular long rows of plain windows, no roof-line or chimneys. Some of the upper windows, it is interesting to note, have been bricked up to narrow slits thus enabling rifle and machine-gun fire to be directed back over the Higham Marshes should an attack be from the land rather than from the sea.

Just beyond is a jetty to receive cargoes of gravel. The pathway leads towards a lengthy continuous rubber belt which builds up huge pyramids of graded building materials. Following

The old wreck near Cliffe Fort

the shoreline due east the path turns inland along Cliffe Creek. The entrance to the creek has been impressively reinforced with Portland stone and concrete. It is a good vantage point to see the expanse of the river all the way back to Gravesend and beyond to Sea reach, across to the oil refinery (a fine industrial landscape floating between sea and sky) and down the creek to its own little boat haven well stocked with pleasure craft. At full tide the creek is unexpectedly broad but it quickly empties leaving only a narrow channel of about 10ft (3m) down the centre.

Quarrying has been extensively carried out in this area. Quarries no longer used have become filled with water and are now virtually lakes. Their sheer sides are shining white and their rugged outlines are covered in tufty grass. Large colonies of birds maintain a continuous hubbub on these 'lakes'. Paths tend to scatter but orientation is easy with the hill of Cliffe village (aptly named) clearly visible on one side in contrast to the spacious flatness of the other. The area is under the preservation of the Kent Wildfowlers Association.

At this point one can continue on to Cliffe for refreshment (there are several pubs and a small shop which is open even on

Sundays) and for a return bus. But if you are planning to return to Gravesend by bus make sure of the times in advance. Cliffe, apart from the old village, is not especially worth a visit. It contains rather a lot of post-war emergency bungalows which now look rather bleak. The original old village, however, is still attractive. Clustered around the parish church, which stands high on a prominent site, it has some nice weatherboarded houses and is approached from the steeply winding lane which runs up from the quarries. However, if you choose to return the way you came you will have the benefit of the mesmerising chimneys of Tilbury Power Station growing with every step and the pleasure of walking into the sunset!

HISTORICAL MONUMENTS ON THE THAMES

17 HMS Belfast – Tower Bridge – Historic Ship Collection – PLA and Trinity House Buildings

This walk includes four sites of outstanding interest which may be fitted into a single walk. It is not of any great distance but there is much to see – so allow plenty of time. However, as each site is so absorbing and worthy of repeated visits individual transport details are given. For the complete walk, follow the sites in the order in which they are given.

HMS Belfast
Trains: London Bridge (underground and British Rail)
Buses: 47, 70 to Tooley Street; buses to London Bridge are numerous
Map: OS sheet no 177

From London Bridge station turn right at Tooley Street and left along Vine Lane where HMS *Belfast* is moored at Symon's Wharf. Once our largest cruiser, it is now a museum (admission charged). She was completed just before the last war and at 11,000 tons was an impressive achievement in the class of fast warships known as cruisers. A cruiser's chief virtue is its mobility and speed to outplay the enemy and to protect convoys. The class-name derives from 'kruisen' meaning 'to cross' and it comes from the Dutch to whom we are indebted for much navigational lore.

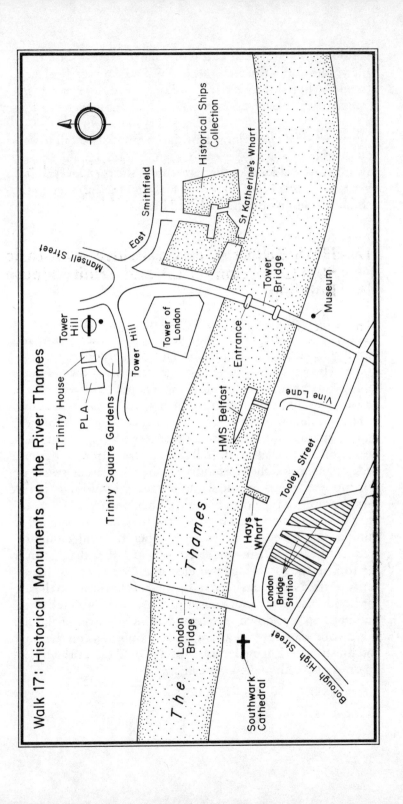

Walk 17: Historical Monuments on the River Thames

HMS *Belfast* is an exhibition of wide interest – not only to agile young boys. The methods of naval warfare are displayed, of course, but so too are the working conditions and living arrangements of professional seamen, and this must interest us all.

From HMS *Belfast* Tower Bridge, with its two tall towers and overhead gangway, is easily seen. On leaving the ship go towards the bridge; take the stairs up to the road level and go over to the north side. Here you will find the entrance to the exhibition (admission charged) and lifts.

Tower Bridge
Trains: Tower Hill underground station
Buses: 42, 78
Map: OS sheet no 177

The traditional crossing of the Thames near the Tower of London was by ferry between Iron Gate Stairs (north side) and Horsleydown Stairs. The first design which proposed the erection of a bridge at this busy crossing was turned down because sailing ships, with their tall masts, would not have been able to pass under it to use the wharfs which were further upstream.

The problem was solved by the brilliant design of the present world-famous bridge: a bascule bridge with huge rising sections which would allow the tall ships to pass through. Because pedestrians would then be hindered when the bascules were up this too was solved by adding an overhead footbridge; it also carred power to the north bascule. When opened in 1894 sailing ships were numerous but by 1910 they had so declined in number that it became necessary to open the bridge only infrequently. Pedestrians preferred to wait rather than go over the top, so the footbridge was closed and remained so for seventy years. Now it has been re-opened. Take the lift to the top for London's finest panoramas. From here the City's tall office buildings are cut down in size and seem less overwhelming. Walk your way down, looking at the exhibitions on the way, and finish in the Engine House Museum on the south bank – all on one ticket. And take your camera.

Historic Ship Collection and St Katharine's Dock
Trains: Tower Hill underground station
Buses: 22a, 23, 42, 78
Map: OS sheet no 177

From the top of Tower Bridge you would have seen, from the north-east corner, the masts of many ships moored in St Katharine's Dock. On returning to road level cross over the bridge to the north-east corner and take the stairs down to the lower level where you immediately turn towards the river. Follow along to the small, white footbridge and follow the path around to the Dickens Inn, a large timber-framed structure. Behind it is the entrance to the Historic Ship Collection of the Maritime Trust.

This Trust serves the interests of old ships in the same way as the National Trust cares for old houses and estates. Established in 1969, the Maritime Trust is a comparative newcomer to preserving our heritage but it has worked wisely and quickly in building up its delightful collection of ships. Those on show at St Katharine's Dock are not only of interest to boat lovers for each ship is, in a sense, a social document of the way part of our society lived and worked in the not too distant past. Collectively they are of exceptional and wide interest.

St Katharine's is a splendid setting. Once the most handsome of our docks – there are superb warehouses of the 1820s by Philip Hardwick – its 'development' has not always fully realised the artistic or historic potential of the site. Fine stretches of water, many glamorous private boats and Hardwick's stupendous clocktower warehouse nevertheless manage to create an air of excitement.

Going over the historic ships (admission charged) is a privilege indeed; we are allowed to scuttle around almost everywhere. See the fish-room in the hold of the fishing boat *Lydia Eva* with its adjustable storage units; the black, iron fuel stove in the galley of the *Nore Lightship*, looking more like 1731 than 1931 when she was built; the rigging, rope ladders, thick knots and marlinspikes of the schooner *Kathleen and May*; Captain Scott's *Discovery* and the *Robin*, last remaining 'dirty British coaster'. After seventy years working for Spanish

Kathleen and May, part of the Historic Ship Collection

owners, she was nearly sent to the breaker's yard but was purchased by the Maritime Trust in 1974, and sailed under her own steam back from Spain.

Port of London Authority and Trinity House
Trains: Tower Hill underground station
Buses: 23, 42, 78
Map: OS sheet no 177

After leaving the previous site, and by going towards Tower Hill station these two buildings dominate the view north of the Tower of London. Though not open for regular inspection, special arrangements might be made by individual applicants.

These two buildings stand side by side on a prominent site just within the eastern limits of the old City walls. Both buildings are important in the history of the Thames and, though utterly different in scale, their common use of Classical motifs and brilliant white stone, draw them together in happy ensemble.

The Port of London Authority was founded under Winston Churchill in 1909 as a much-needed organisation to administer the enormous trade of London's port. Sir Edwin Cooper, an Edwardian virtuoso of the commercial style, handled the daunting brief and rose to the artistic occasion. Although begun in 1912, construction was interrupted by World War I and was not completed until 1922. Surmounting this great structure is a grandiose tower; a muscular Neptune with Roman galleons at his feet and charioteers either side adorns the upper structure. At ground level there are magnificent bronze lamp standards. But time passes, and in 1971 the Authority sold the building to insurance brokers and moved out to Tilbury.

The comparative miniature which is Trinity House holds its own by its sheer charm and elegance. Built in 1794 to the design of Samuel Wyatt, its handsome features are an expression of the natural good sense and consciousness of men who put to sea. Trinity House is responsible for pilotage, lighthouses and sea-marks. Though severely damaged during the last war, the fact that it is largely a restoration is undetectable.

OTHER THINGS TO DO AND SEE

River Buses
Westminster Pier: Westminster underground station
Buses: 12, 53 and 70 stop nearest to the pier but the choice to
nearby stops is enormous
Tower Pier: Tower Hill underground station
Buses:23, 42, 78
Map: OS sheet no 177

Journeys to Greenwich by attractive passenger boats continue
throughout the year from Westminster Pier and Tower Pier. It
is a half-hourly service. Going down river you pass (north
bank) the former riverside villages of murder and smuggling
fame: Wapping, Shadwell, Ratcliff and Limehouse. Now the
monolithic warehouses are converted to homes for the
wealthy. For two hundred years, from mid-eighteenth to
mid-twentieth century, the world's greatest port occupied
these reaches of the Thames.

From April to October there are services upriver from
Westminster Pier to Putney, Kew, Richmond and Hampton
Court. The journey to Hampton Court is a wonderful day on
the river. The journey alone takes three to four hours in each
direction. It passes first through areas of dense urban building
and a fine succession of bridges and then on past typically
English rural scenery in a number of great parks: Barnes
Common, Kew Gardens, Syon Park, Richmond Park, Marble
Hill Park and Hampton Court Park. All the time the Thames
decreases in width which adds to the impression of having
made a long journey.

Greenwich

Greenwich oozes with riverine history. Once its medieval palace was the favoured home of Tudor monarchs – Henry VIII was born there, as were Mary I and Elizabeth I. Now all interest is centred upon two historic ships, *Cutty Sark* and *Gypsy Moth*, the Royal Naval College, the National Maritime Museum and that indispensable meridian for navigators the world over, Greenwich Observatory. Getting there and seeing it all is a wonderful experience but it is a long day so start early.

Go by boat from Westminster or Tower Piers. Or try the Docklands Clipper (Monday to Saturday) which commenced service at the beginning of 1984. This bus, the D1, leaves from Mile End Road underground station (Burdett Road stop) and winds round through the West India and Millwall Docks giving fine views of these once busy centres of shipping. Get off at Manchester Road and cut through to the River Thames (right) and to Island Gardens. From here you get the finest view, across the water, of the great Baroque palace of the Royal Naval College. The large rotunda in the gardens is the entrance to Greenwich Tunnel (1902), a marvellous echoing footway running under the Thames and taking you to Greenwich. After your visit return to London by boat.

The *Cutty Sark,* a Scottish phrase meaning 'short shirt', was a speedy tea clipper which worked from 1869 to 1922. The exquisite springing curve of her deck tells of the lithe way she must have dealt with the ocean's waves. Below decks there is an interesting exhibition of marine illustrations and carved figureheads from old sailing ships (admission charged).

Gypsy Moth is a tribute to a courageous twentieth-century adventurer. In 1967 Francis Chichester completed his round-the-world voyage in her single-handed in nine months. His homecoming was received with unprecedented publicity and enthusiasm. There had been nothing to compare with his achievement since Drake's. Appropriately, both were knighted by Elizabethan queens who used the same sword. Open April to October (admission charged).

The Royal Naval College (Wren 1702) is the greatest setpiece in this country: formal grounds flanked by twin colonnaded terraces, symmetrically placed domes to mark the Chapel and the Painted Hall and, central to all, the chaste Palladianism of the Queen's House (Inigo Jones 1640). Everything is, to use Inigo's phrase, 'proporsionable [sic] according to the rules'.

The National Maritime Museum (free admission) incorporates the Queen's House and the Royal Observatory. The collection is wide ranging and full of unexpected things of interest, such as the utterly absorbing and beautiful chronometers. The collection of river barges, with their tasselled and gilded cabins, reveals the pageantry of private transport for the privileged of old.

The Royal Observatory was founded in 1675 by the first Astronomer Royal, John Flamsteed, with the support of that most enlightened king, Charles II. Developments over nearly three hundred years placed Greenwich firmly in peoples' minds, perhaps the world over, when the meridian was established in 1884.

Scientific work at the Observatory was transferred to the clear air of Herstmonceaux after the last war; even so, the collection of instruments at the present museum offers research enough for the fastidious student and wonder for those who can but admire.

The Thames Barrier
Trains: Charlton (British Rail)
Buses: 51, 96, 161, 177, 180
Map: OS sheet no 177

Within the vicinity of the Thames in London there are large areas of land which are actually below high-water level, testifying to the river's changing course over the centuries. Altogether, the low-lying land of Bexley, Barking, Newham, Greenwich, Tower Hamlets, Southwark, Lambeth and Westminster comes to an astonishing 24sq miles (62sq km), with a further danger zone of 21sq miles (54sq km). A serious flooding of London would require the simultaneous occurrence of several major weather conditions: an exceptionally high tide and gale force winds blowing from a north-easterly direction. Such conditions would force additional water into the Estuary to increase further the high-water level and, as the river narrows on its way to London, the funnelling effect would result in a deluge. It has happened on many occasions in the past.

The Thames Barrier and its attendant system of flood walls and barriers on the creeks at Bow, Barking and Dartford are intended to hold back water levels of this sort. The Barrier was officially opened by the Queen in May 1984 although it had by then been in operation for eighteen months.

The structure consists of nine enormous piers spaced across the river at Woolwich. Between them there are rotating gates which may be opened by setting them in a position where they are lying on the river bed, or closed by raising them into vertical positions thus holding back the water. If need be, all gates may be closed thereby holding back the almighty forces of wind and tide.

The engineers of this great project were Rendel, Palmer and Tritton. Founded a hundred and fifty years ago by the distinguished engineer James Meadows Rendel, this firm has been associated with major projects throughout the world: docks, harbours, bridges, highways and railways, especially the construction of the Indian railways during the days of the British Raj.

The most attractive feature of the design arose from the idea of the GLC Architects Department to house the hydraulic gate-operating machinery in stainless steel domes. They are beautifully conceived. The small steel plates which form the skin have a rippled surface which reflects a soft irridescent glow while the dome shape itself, influenced by the Sydney Opera House, suggests both the prow of a boat and a sail. The cost of the barrier came to £400 million, but in addition an equivalent sum was spent on the construction of flood defence walls which were built upstream to raise the level of the banks on either side.

Launching Site: the Isle of Dogs
The Thames has been transformed in recent years from a poisonous channel to a clean salmon-breeding river. The upper reaches were always popular for boating and sailing but now the interest has extended to the metropolitan reaches as well.

Without a permanent mooring site downstream, however, it is difficult to know how to explore London's Thames.

An excellent public launching site exists at the southern tip of the Isle of Dogs. It is at the end of Glenaffric Avenue E14, a turning off the ring road which runs round the peninsula. It is clearly visible on a street map. The site is always open, but un-attended, and has ample room for parking cars and trailers. A pub is on the corner.

A concrete slipway is provided though launching and recovery are not possible at low tide. All types of boats use the site, including canoes, and water-skiing is popular. Anybody with their own craft can enjoy the rich social and architectural treasures of the London Thames from this site – Greenwich, after all, is just across the river.

FURTHER READING

Anderson, Jo. *Anchor and Hope* (Hodder & Stoughton, 1980)
Barton, Nicholas. *The Lost Rivers of London* (Historical Publications, 1982)
Borer, Mary Cathcart. *The City of London* (Constable, 1977)
Brandon, Peter. *A History of Surrey* (Phillimore, 1977)
Cove-Smith, Chris. *London's Waterway Guide* (Imray Laurie, 1977)
Cracknell, Basil. *Portrait of London's River* (Hale, 1968)
Holme, Thea. *Chelsea* (Hamish Hamilton, 1972)
Phillips, Geoffrey. *Thames Crossings* (David & Charles, 1981)
Pudney, John. *London's Docks* (Thames and Hudson, 1975)

INDEX

171